— AUTOGRAPHED BY THE AUTHOR —

LEAP

"Full of practical tools and real-world insights for making that next leap forward." —STEVE FORBES

LEAP

MASTER YOUR SUPERPOWERS, SOAR TO THE LEADING EDGE

DR. MARTA WILSON

ForbesBooks

Published by ForbesBooks, Charleston, South Carolina.
Member of Advantage Media Group.

ForbesBooks is a registered trademark, and the ForbesBooks colophon is a trademark of Forbes Media, LLC.

Printed in the United States of America.

10 9 8 7 6 5 4 3 2 1

ISBN: 978-1-94663-365-1
LCCN: 2019913892

Book design by Carly Blake.

This publication is designed to provide accurate and authoritative information in regard to the subject matter covered. It is sold with the understanding that the publisher is not engaged in rendering legal, accounting, or other professional services. If legal advice or other expert assistance is required, the services of a competent professional person should be sought.

Advantage Media Group is proud to be a part of the Tree Neutral® program. Tree Neutral offsets the number of trees consumed in the production and printing of this book by taking proactive steps such as planting trees in direct proportion to the number of trees used to print books. To learn more about Tree Neutral, please visit **www.treeneutral.com**.

Since 1917, the Forbes mission has remained constant. Global Champions of Entrepreneurial Capitalism. ForbesBooks exists to further that aim by bringing the Stories, Passion, and Knowledge of top thought leaders to the forefront. ForbesBooks brings you The Best in Business. To be considered for publication, please visit **www.forbesbooks.com**.

For Donny and Danny, my wonderful brothers.
Since childhood, you've been my superheroes.
I love you.

and

In memory of Captain Bob, my one true love.
You'll be forever in my heart.
1955-2019

CONTENTS

PREFACE

Would you like to take yourself to the next level at work, home, or in some other area of your life? Why do some people with equal talent, education, and experience soar while others seem to falter? Success in life and in work requires strategy and motivation … as well as tapping into your own unique superpowers to master the skills of effective leadership.

But how do you choose to take a leap rather than simply stumble? And how does that act transform into an ability to soar, to appear at ease and in control, confident enough to defy gravity and take flight? How do you not only make a commitment to improving your life but then maintain that commitment for the long haul?

Life is stressful, and people have limited time to develop effective leadership skills in a more complex and competitive world. And let's face it: effective leadership often requires changing how we do things, and change can be difficult. But as effective people and as leaders, we must be bold as we face the challenges that come with change. Boldness requires stepping into the unknown.

In 2002, when I launched my company, Transformation Systems, Inc. (TSI), I made an investment: in myself, in my beliefs, in my ideas about how great organizations operate and how they succeed. I left an academic job for an adventure into the unknown. My intention was to build a company of possibility thinkers—of superheroes—who would help leaders achieve their boldest goals. I invested by making a lot of personal sacrifices. I took risks. I asked people who already had good jobs and were on solid career trajectories to become my employees. It was difficult for me to ask them to take such a risk. Why would they want to step off the cliff into the abyss with me, trusting my vision and absolute belief in what I intended to build?

But guess what? They took the leap with me.

And now, almost two decades later, TSI has shared our message with thousands of people in organizations ranging from federal agencies to *Fortune* 500 companies. We consult with these organizations to help them uncover the hidden gifts of executives, managers, and employees to build morale, increase collaboration, and enhance success. Our work includes achieving transformation goals such as reducing costs, increasing efficiency, and energizing the workforce. With this book, I want to extend to you the message and work that TSI has already shared with thousands of others. Within its pages you will find the keys to achieving your own transformational goals and unveiling your superpowers.

PEOPLE WHO ARE MASTERFUL IN THE FOUR AREAS THAT ARE THE FOCUS OF THIS BOOK TEND TO BECOME SUPERHEROES.

Now more than ever, people want and need to know the best proven practices to help them thrive. What I've discovered throughout my career—both as an academic and as a consultant—is that my experience working with organizations and the research about them match: people who are masterful in the four areas that are the focus of this book tend to become superheroes, those whom others rely on to lead the way forward when things are at risk of falling apart.

LEAP reveals a path to soar to the leading edge by strengthening four kinds of mastery. Mastery, in my use of the word, means demonstrating the ability to think, decide, and act effectively in each of the following four areas:

1. **PERSONAL**
2. **INTERPERSONAL**
3. **ORGANIZATIONAL**
4. **MOTIVATIONAL**

These four types of mastery make up the Leadership Effectiveness And Potential (LEAP) model, a system for establishing more impactful leadership, which I've developed over the course of more than thirty years of research and consultation. LEAP has helped thousands of people improve their professional and personal success. And it can help you, too.

In this user-friendly guide, you'll get acquainted with the LEAP Profile (which you will find in chapter 3), which helps you easily evaluate your personal, interpersonal, organizational, and motivational skills. This book also provides the necessary tools to move toward mastery in all four areas. In addition, I've developed the LEAP app so that you have a portable tool available on your phone to explore these concepts in more depth. The app is available at theLEAPapp.com.

Like the app, this book is a fast-paced crash course in proven principles of individual effectiveness and is filled with guidance from science and industry on how to build personal, interpersonal, organizational, and motivational mastery. Alongside this proven advice on how to activate your superpowers, throughout the book you'll find inspirational examples of great leaders at work in sections titled "Mastery in Action." There you will meet business leaders, celebrities, politicians, and coaches who demonstrate the principles of LEAP.

In addition to my own story, I'll guide you through

the experiences of some of my past and present clients who demonstrate how mastery in these areas has led to success on a scale they once only imagined.

If you choose to put these facts, tips, and solutions in motion, you will not only become a better leader, but you will exponentially magnify your impact as you inspire and guide your friends, family, and colleagues to unleash their potential and reach higher crests of performance now and into the future. Are you ready to take your next step toward new peaks of performance?

1

IMAGINE YOURSELF SOARING

When I launched Transformation Systems, Inc. (TSI) in 2002 as a full-time endeavor, I faced many daunting unknowns. TSI had been set up as a side gig years earlier, after I completed my PhD, to allow me to do professional activity on top of my full-time academic job. But, in 2002, I made the complete break from an academic career to a business one. I had never run a company before, and I knew I had a lot to learn. To be successful, TSI would need to develop relationships with large enterprises, including government agencies, but I didn't know if I would be accepted as the right authority who could provide them the help they needed. People I deeply admired had shifted their career trajectories to help me build TSI, and I had yet to master and refine many of the skills required to be an effective CEO who could turn my desire to help leaders reach their full potential into a meaningful, moneymaking enterprise. Many times, I asked myself, "What am I doing?"

When I admitted to my colleagues that I had this dream—but was also nervous, because I didn't *know* if I could pull it off—they rallied to my side and offered their support and expertise. My vulnerability actually helped me. I allowed them to see the full range of my emotions including my excitement, courage, and apprehension. I told them how much I believed in them and wanted them on my team. And I made sure they understood I cared about each of them deeply.

Not only did my willingness to be vulnerable and ask for help win me some extraordinary business partners, it also revealed the unfailing support of my spouse. I put our house on the line, went without paychecks, and emptied my savings account; I was not going to give up.

And yes, I had some regrets the first few years. After all, I'd come from a university background and didn't realize the amount of infrastructure—IT equipment and support, health and liability insurance, trademarks of intellectual property, to name just a few—I'd have to create to make TSI work. But I learned, I grew, and I asked for help.

Seventeen years later, TSI is a highly respected and award-winning firm that helps organizations and individuals build more effective and powerful systems for change, opportunity, and sustainability. And I've personally had the opportunity, as a CEO and industrial-organizational psychologist, to coach, speak, and write about transformational leadership around the world—in Scotland, Singapore, South Africa, Botswana, Canada, Mexico, and throughout the United States. In all my travels and all my endeavors, I have focused on helping leaders discover and apply their powers to transform the people and systems around them.

The TSI team has helped clients set historic records in the speed of Department of Defense (DoD) acquisition processes and also facilitated large-scale technology transitions. For five consecutive years, we've ranked on the Inc. 5000 list for fastest-growing private companies in America and also been recognized by *Washington Business Journal* as one of the Best Places to Work. The journal also recognized me as one of the Top 25 Women Business Leaders in Washington, DC. And we've done it all by helping people, one-on-one and in groups, achieve new levels of leadership effectiveness.

Seeing TSI grow has been humbling. It all unfolded as I took chances, dared to be vulnerable, and demonstrated curiosity. In essence, I stepped out of my comfort zone. You can, too.

CALL YOUR INNER SUPERHERO

As with the superheroes you may have admired as a child, success will require vaulting over really tall obstacles and having faith that, with the right tools, you can soar like they did. But you can't soar unless you first leap. LEAP stands for Leadership Effectiveness And Potential. The LEAP program includes assessments, keynotes, workshops, training, mentoring, learning reinforcers such as the LEAP app, and ongoing consulting and transformation support. Within the LEAP framework, four types of mastery help us advance to the leading edge of performance:

1. **PERSONAL MASTERY**

   Exercising commitment, curiosity, and courage to become the best version of ourselves we can possibly be.

2. **INTERPERSONAL MASTERY**

   Connecting, communicating, and collaborating with others to achieve individual and organizational goals.

3. **ORGANIZATIONAL MASTERY**

   Understanding the people, processes, and products

within our work environments and how they're all connected in supplying our customers with exactly what they need at exactly the right time.

4. **MOTIVATIONAL MASTERY**

   Engaging, elevating, and energizing those around us so they, too, strive to be their best selves and unite with others to reach important missions.

I consistently use the term "mastery" throughout the book, for that's truly what we're after. It's like the traditional craftsman system for artists, stonemasons, and carpenters, among others, where one apprenticed oneself to a master and completed the learning process by becoming a journeyman and ultimately a master. There you learned specific skills and techniques, whereas here, as you continue your leadership journey, you will work with intention toward mastery of the beliefs, approaches, knowledge, and actions that will allow you to expand your results, leverage your relationships, integrate the elements of your work environment, and inspire improved performance in those around you. Mastery in all the four areas of the LEAP model advances us toward the leading edge of effectiveness.

To approach the leading edge of effectiveness, one important step is to recognize there is an order to the LEAP model. Each of the four masteries build upon one another. For example, it's difficult to possess the necessary skills of interpersonal mastery—connecting, communicating, and collaborating with others—until we have mastered our ability to be responsible for our own results, an element of personal mastery. Have you ever had a boss who lacked the courage to lead or suffered from low self-confidence (and perhaps masked low self-esteem by belittling others)? If you have, then you've seen how such a person is incapable of leading a collaborative, vision-driven team. Leaders cannot develop the integrative needs of motivating and working with others until they consistently display commitment to self-improvement, the courage to step beyond what they already know and what makes them comfortable, and curiosity about ideas, processes, and people. Each of the masteries helps develop the skills required to reach the next. But, feel free to determine your own starting point and jump in.

Much of this book will not only explain and clarify why mastery within the four quadrants of the LEAP model matters to becoming a successful leader, but it also shares valuable lessons on how to become masterful. Along the way, you'll see some of the steps—and meet some of the mentors—that have helped me hone who I am today. This is true in large part because I've been honest about following my own advice and have been intentional in my development as a leader. Like everyone else, I've made mistakes along the way and put the lessons from those mistakes to work. By combining the quest for my own development with my academic background in psychology and with the experience of running a company that serves multibillion-dollar enterprises, I've boosted my own Leadership Effectiveness And Potential. I made the LEAP.

Along my journey, I've seen what you've seen (or you probably wouldn't be reading this book):

- individuals who had lost their drive and edge, who were going through the motions rather than being enthused about their enterprises or their roles within them;
- poor leaders ineffective at communicating with their teams.;
- convoluted processes mired in purposeless bureaucracy that had lost sight of the actual mission; and
- unhappy, stifling workplaces where work had become nothing more than … well … work.

LEAP helps rudderless organizations and the people who are so earnestly trying to steer them. Some of us want nothing more than the appearance of some superhuman being drafted out of the comic book pages to fly in, apply extraneous strength, and put the crashing plane back on course. Those sorts of superheroes only exist in comic books and in the movies. The real-life versions look exactly like you and me, and when we master the lessons of LEAP, we boost our superpowers. And you can master them. The core concepts are not difficult in theory, though they take real commitment to apply consistently in our lives.

FIRST STEPS TOWARD SUPERHERO POWERS

We must first establish a commitment to ourselves. This is no easy task. There is no one in the workforce today who doesn't struggle, at least from time to time, with commitment to self—mind, body, spirit, and values. It's a struggle. You must take care of yourself before you can grow as a leader and take care of and inspire others. Without commitment there can be no mastery. Self-commitment is the starting point. But how do you get there?

PART OF BEING A SUPERHERO IS NOTICING THOSE AROUND YOU AND MENTORING THEM TO BE SUPERHEROES, TOO.

STEP 1: Understand you *are* a superhero to someone. Maybe it's to your child. Maybe it's to an intern in the office. Part of being a superhero is noticing those around you and mentoring them to be superheroes, too.

STEP 2: Recognize that to soar, to unleash your

inner superhero, you must evolve. An inherent part of the commitment I am asking you to make is twofold: to evaluate where you are in your leadership development now and to accept the need for transformation. And by nature, whether we're talking about Clark Kent becoming Superman or Diana Prince turning into Wonder Woman, transformation means a willingness to let go of your fear of change and your acceptance of the status quo.

STEP 3: Superpowers are amplified with clear intention. When I talk about intention, I always say, where there's a will, there's a way. What is will? Will is intention. If I want clear intention, I get focused on my goal with such unbending purpose that I refuse to fail, no matter what.

For example, imagine receiving a phone call at work to learn that a close family member needs you immediately. It's an emergency. Would you go? What if you had a critical deadline to meet? What if your coworker locked you in the building? What if you made it to the parking lot but your car wouldn't start? Every time I describe this situation, the response is consistent. People visualize doing whatever it takes to reach their loved one. This is an example of clear intention.

Our results are related to the intentions that preceded them. Success requires that we get clear about the results we choose to create. Imagine you are habitually late and declare to the world that from now on you will be on time. But, the following day you're ten minutes late for work. What do you blame? What's your excuse? Perhaps heavy traffic or a broken alarm clock. These are common ten-minute excuses. Now, imagine that the next day you show up four hours late. So, you need a four-hour story. A four-hour excuse might involve a flat tire or a plumbing leak. And then, what if you don't show up for a week? You'd better have an Oscar-worthy performance to explain yourself when you do resurface!

Think about this: What would happen if you were guaranteed to receive a million dollars in cash for showing up on time at work? What would you do to ensure you weren't late? You might leave from home at three o'clock in the morning, arrive at work, park, and sit in your car until the doors open. You might camp out overnight on the front steps of your office building. You might even handcuff yourself to your office chair and refuse to leave the building at all! My point is, when we are clear about what we want, we will find a way to be it, do it, or have it. When we have the will to achieve an outcome, we can discover the way to make that outcome a reality. Finding the WAY to make things happen lies in our WILL, not in blaming outside forces.

How do we clarify our intention? We focus like a laser with unbending purpose. We define what we want. Most people are conscious about what they don't want. The challenge is to get conscious about what we DO want. Being successful demands clarity about what we want for ourselves—what we want to be, do, and have.

Overall, what do *you* want to be, do, and have? Personally, I'm on a mission to be my best, do great things, and have meaningful success. Our success hinges on the clarity of our answers to this question. This is true at home, at work, and in all areas of our lives. Clear intention starts with what you want.

COMFORT ZONES CAN BECOME OUR KRYPTONITE

Let's talk a little more about what can hold us back as we pursue mastery and success. On the one hand, we know there's probably a better way to achieve some of our goals than what we're doing right now. On the other hand, we can be distracted from implementing new strategies because we're so busy fighting fires at work and at home every day. We have deadlines to meet, internal processes to navigate, an inbox that's bursting at the seams, and a steady stream of voice mails. You may feel like you are what's holding everything together. But you want more than that, don't you?

Getting more, however, requires getting uncomfortable.

Maintaining the status quo isn't going to work in

helping us achieve big, long-term goals. That can be a very tough thing to accept. We must be prepared to let go of comfort in order to be more effective as people and leaders. When faced with the chance to expand our comfort zones, however, we must exert our will over our habits and consciously *choose* to behave in new ways.

Change is uncomfortable. That's why our native tendency is to entrench ourselves in comfort zones. A comfort zone has been described as "a behavioral state within which a person operates in an anxiety-neutral position."[1] It's where we function and still feel in control.

Comfort zones aren't always bad. Driving at one hundred miles per hour down a winding road would make most of us feel anxious and afraid, as it should. Staying in the comfort zone of the speed limit keeps us safe and protects us from bodily injury.

But when we're talking about leadership and making things happen, comfort zones can hold us back. If we choose comfort over growth, we ultimately may be opting for the greater risk.[2] Sometimes we need to speak up even when doing so makes us uncomfortable. Sometimes we simply need to be willing to say no when conformity provides the habit of saying yes. Comfort zones, if left unquestioned, can also limit leaders and even harm them and their organizations by resulting in decreased profits, lower employee morale, and lack of customer satisfaction. Yet "the reality in many organizations today is that despite the public emphasis on innovation, the underlying culture may be strongly risk-averse,"[3] something that is true even when innovation may be required for growth or staying relevant in a changing world.

SUCCESSFUL AND INFLUENTIAL PEOPLE STEP OUTSIDE THEIR COMFORT ZONES. THEY ARE WILLING TO EXPERIMENT, TRY NEW METHODS, AND EVEN RISK FAILURE.

Successful and influential people step outside their comfort zones. They are willing to experiment, try new methods, and even risk failure. It is this push to grow, even if growth means risking failure, that is a cornerstone supporting all the masteries that are at the heart of this book. To be on the leading edge, we must continuously grow. Aside from the *words* that make up LEAP—Leadership Effectiveness And Potential—the *metaphor* behind "leap" suggests an intentional commitment to change. As psychology will remind us, humans do not naturally embrace change. We must *choose* it.

As I've already alluded, the reason this book is in your hands has a lot to do with my own efforts at experimentation in order to accomplish meaningful change in my life and in my role as a leader. I've stopped imagining I will stumble into a personal version of kryptonite and have chosen to take many risks. You'll read a lot about my own development, even about some of my own fears. In the "Mastery in Action" sections of this book, which focus on accomplished people who have crossed my path and have become teachers and mentors on the traits needed to lead effectively, I'm also telling my own story of growth and intentional change.

If you had asked me twenty-five years ago if I saw myself writing a series of books on leadership effectiveness, I might have laughed. Yet in 2005, I began working on *Leaders in Motion*, and it was in writing that book (which dives into personal and interpersonal mastery) that I started putting meat on the bones of the LEAP model.

Then, I decided I needed to push myself a little harder. So, I wrote two more books: *Everybody's Business* and *Energized Enterprise*. The three books became a trilogy addressing the entire LEAP model. Today, that trilogy is a critical part of the program my team members at TSI lead for global organizations, in part because I pushed myself to write books and tell my own story.

THROUGH THE LENS OF SCIENCE:
Discovering the Fountain of Youth

Here's a welcome fact: scientific research has demonstrated that trying new things and getting out of your comfort zone actually preserves your brain from the effects of aging. Lisa Feldman Barrett, a university distinguished professor of psychology at Northeastern University, set out to discover why some people remain mentally nimble as they age while others decline. She states,

> Superagers (a term coined by the neurologist Marsel Mesulam) are those whose memory and attention isn't merely above average for their age, but is actually on par with healthy, active twenty-five-year-olds. My colleagues and I at Massachusetts General Hospital recently studied superagers to understand what made them tick.[4]

Barrett discovered that,

> Many labs have observed that these critical brain regions increase in activity when people perform difficult tasks, whether the effort is physical or mental. You can therefore help keep these regions thick and healthy through vigorous exercise and bouts of strenuous mental effort.[5]

Such research has led to the growth industry of phone applications and mental performance games for those trying to stave off the effects of aging. More importantly for our interests, the act of trying new things—whether that is picking up the guitar, learning a language, practicing yoga, or taking on new responsibilities at work—all stimulate increased activity in these critical brain regions.

SUPERHEROES LEARN TO FACE THEIR FEARS

Another aspect of stepping out of comfort zones is creating tolerance for approaching things we fear, something psychologists discuss with the language of "approach-avoidance" when discussing interaction with conflict. Most people are willing to change, and everyone is ready for some degree of change, even if it's very small. At the same time, however, people fear the consequences of change and what they might lose during and after. This is a classic approach-avoidance conflict. It occurs when we're attracted to and repelled by a goal at the same time. Perhaps you've been offered a promotion and a pay raise. You know it comes with greater responsibility, more work, and a higher level of stress, so you want the promotion. However, part of you also *doesn't* want it because the change it imposes on your life makes you fearful.

I had that approach-avoidance conflict experience myself when I launched TSI as a full-time endeavor. I wanted to lead my own company, but at the same time, I was nervous and not initially convinced I could do it and be successful. I chose to face that fear head on, however, and strive to do what I'd always wanted to do … leave academia and establish a company filled with possibility thinkers who helped transformational leaders emerge and excel.

We may yearn to rise to the occasion and achieve audacious goals in new and compelling ways. But we're also afraid of what might go wrong, looking foolish, and being out of control. I certainly lived with that kind of fear in the initial years of TSI's launch and growth. Yet most people are ready to approach change, just as I was, because they can see the advantage and fulfillment that will come if they prove successful. Are you one of them? Can your yearning overcome your hesitation?

It's human nature to experience the approach-avoidance conflict when faced with the opportunity to change the status quo. But effective people find ways to make the *goal* of change more attractive than the *fear* of change.

When we understand that approach-avoidance is natural, we can learn to embrace it and choose experimentation over stagnation.

LEADERS WHO SOAR

Through experimentation, we can become transformational leaders. Transformational leadership is something that has drawn my interest since I was in graduate school. I knew when I went out into the workforce, I wanted to help transformational leaders be their best, do great things, and have meaningful success—to help those who would influence and drive change within their organizations. In fact, that's why my company is named Transformation Systems.

As leaders, we are called upon to be change agents, both within our organizations and in our broader lives. We strive to create environments that inspire performance and boost the effectiveness of those around us.

With a deep interest in the subject, I studied transformational leadership theory, which posits that leaders who have the biggest impact and drive the most results share common traits. Transformational leaders not only have a positive impact on the performance of others; they motivate others to perform beyond their perceived abilities.

Transformational leaders influence their employees' engagement, inclusion, and involvement in a positive way. My experience has been that employees of transformational leaders feel they have a lot of variety, significance, and autonomy in their careers. They also tend to be high performers.

How do you become a transformational leader? You must become comfortable seizing opportunities as they present themselves and setting an example for continuous self-improvement. As you challenge yourself to learn and grow, you'll find those within your sphere of influence will do the same.

Transformational leaders drive and enable quantifiable outcomes, including increased employee engagement, performance, and satisfaction. They understand employees' needs and help them feel understood and appreciated. This results in a strong emotional bond between the leader and his or her team, which in turn inspires greater team effort and performance.

MASTERY IN ACTION:
My Nephew Leaps and Soars

A few years ago, I was in the Outer Banks of North Carolina with my family, and one evening I sat on the deck and talked for a long time with my nephew, Max. He was preparing for his senior year in high school, and we were talking about his dreams for the future. When I asked Max where he wanted to go in life, he said, "Aunt Marta, I've decided I want to be a naval aviator."

He added, "I want to be a naval officer because leaders in the Navy are some of the most disciplined, professional people in the world. And they have true integrity." Quite a statement for a seventeen-year-old!

Max had been interested in flying since an early age. In fact, he had his pilot's license before his driver's license. After experiencing Max's enthusiasm and drive, I became invested in his dream and was profoundly moved when, a few years later, I attended Max's naval commissioning and his college graduation at Carnegie Mellon University. A newly commissioned ensign, Max entered the naval flight-training pipeline and was soon selected to be a member of the Strike community. He has learned to land F-18 Super Hornets on aircraft carriers and is now a skilled fighter pilot who serves his country with discipline, professionalism, and integrity.

Max had a big dream, and the determination to fulfill it. As an emerging leader, he is soaring and building his personal, interpersonal, organizational, and motivational mastery. Frankly, Max inspired and motivated me to take some new and exciting risks of my own!

BRINGING IT ALL TOGETHER

We can all dream of soaring to new heights, and we can choose to rise higher. But it's important to remember that everyone's path is different, and everyone has his or her own unique potential. In this book, I'll help you identify and cultivate that potential. It's something you can do whether you've recently entered your field or feel you've seen it all through a long career. *LEAP* shares a holistic and scientific approach grounded in research and practice that will not only address many of your challenges before they start to interfere with your success but also will help you lift the people around you to higher levels of satisfaction and performance.

Questions for Reflection, Discovery, and Action

1. What do I dream of being, doing, and having in my life? What have I achieved already in these areas?
2. What new experiences might I seek out in order to grow, develop, and expand my horizons?
3. What are my comfort zones and where do I feel safest and most competent?
4. What might my life look like if I took more risks?
5. What experiences or challenges do I want to tackle yet also fear approaching?
6. What are some specific actions I can take *today* to step out of my comfort zones?

2

GET TO KNOW YOUR MASTERIES

When I was six years old, my parents moved my twin brothers and me from Hawkins County in rural Tennessee to Morristown, a town of about forty thousand people near Knoxville. Growing up as farmers, my parents never had much money, but they believed that in moving to a more populous area and finding jobs in town, they would enhance future prospects for my brothers and me.

My dad had not graduated from high school, my mom was very sick with a chronic condition that required ongoing medical treatment, and we were underinsured. My parents worried about us going into debt to pay medical bills. They also dreamed of buying us a nice home one day. It would have been easy for them to think our prospects looked very dim. But my parents had a vision of prosperity, and they were committed to achieving it.

As a family, we scrimped and saved. We lived in a tiny rental. On weekends, while my school friends were taking swimming lessons and doing other fun things, I would travel fifty miles with my family across Clinch Mountain to my mother's family farm to plant and grow our food. I didn't step inside a restaurant until I was a teenager. My mother and aunts made my clothes, or I wore hand-me-downs from my older cousins.

Despite the challenges and hard work, my dad always found ways to motivate us and make life fun. He was a leader who knew his own mind, had a plan for his goals, and was able to continually encourage and inspire my mom, my brothers, and me. He went for it and challenged himself to pursue his dreams, and he was innately curious. Growing up, I experienced hardship mixed with love and learned that even if you're in the humblest of circumstances, you can thrive, build something from nothing, and expand your horizons.

I looked up to my father as a kind of superhero. He always fulfilled those expectations. Looking back, I now realize that in the heroic qualities I admired, my dad exhibited mastery, the very types of mastery that would one day become the LEAP model. Dad never became a high-profile executive, but he eventually helped my family achieve our goals, because he was laser-focused on achieving a dream. He was personally, interpersonally, and organizationally masterful. *And,* he motivated us.

There's a reason people like my dad achieve challenging goals against insurmountable odds. And you can do the same, no matter what your current circumstances and no matter what your field of work.

THERE'S A REASON PEOPLE LIKE MY DAD ACHIEVE CHALLENGING GOALS AGAINST INSURMOUNTABLE ODDS. AND YOU CAN DO THE SAME.

What my father demonstrated was mastery: the ability to think, decide, and act effectively. Mastery invokes powerful images of moving quickly and easily, exhibiting nimbleness and intellectual acuity, and exercising the ability to think and draw conclusions rapidly. Mastery allows one to create results and adapt to different situations with ease.

MASTERY: THE ABILITY TO THINK, DECIDE, AND ACT EFFECTIVELY.

LEAP gives access to that mastery, providing a framework that highlights the value of being intentionally balanced. It offers new ways of thinking about how we can leverage ourselves and others to facilitate stronger individual and group performance.

Before we dig deep and explore each of the four areas of mastery—personal, interpersonal, organizational, and motivational—let's first overview all four and look at how we can use them to expand our results, leverage our relationships, integrate our environment, and inspire others' performance.

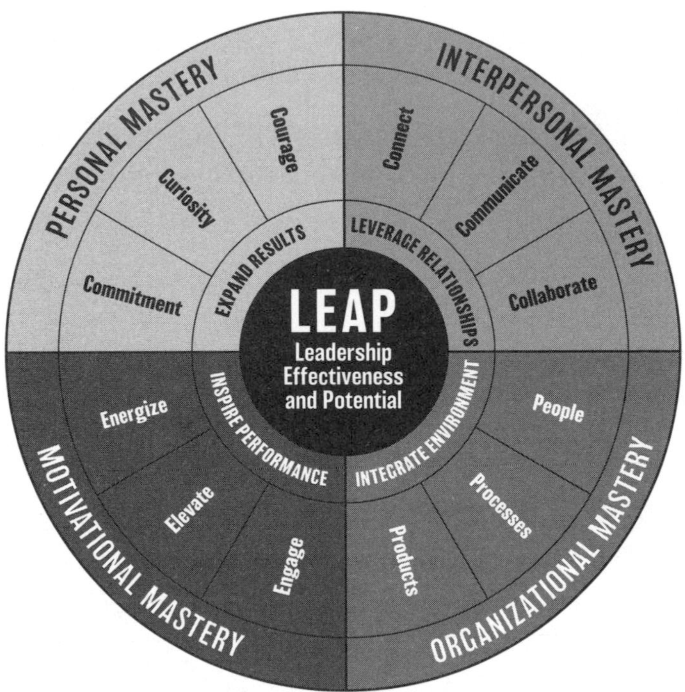

THE LEADERSHIP EFFECTIVENESS AND POTENTIAL (LEAP) MODEL

THROUGH THE LENS OF SCIENCE:
The Origins of LEAP

Well before launching my company, and well before developing LEAP, I was an academic, completing my PhD in industrial-organizational psychology.

The foundational bedrock of LEAP began with my doctoral dissertation. Under the typically daunting title expected by academic research, which craves precision, my dissertation was titled "Manager-Subordinate Exchange Relationships: Investigation of a Manager Behavior Model." The study I designed and led involved 292 manager-subordinate dyads from eighteen work groups in a manufacturing plant. They were observed by a team of trained research assistants for many hours, and they completed questionnaires.

I analyzed the data collected from observations of manager behaviors as defined within our discipline and their subordinates' absence rates. I also investigated managers' and subordinates' perceptions of subordinates' satisfaction, including, among other measures, their satisfaction with their supervisor, growth satisfaction, work satisfaction, coworker satisfaction alongside the subordinates' perception of their own intent to withdraw, and how much negotiating latitude they possessed in the relationship.

The study revealed significant relationships between negotiating latitude with satisfaction, turnover, and absenteeism. These results offered me a first glimpse into how the perceptions of people toward their bosses colored relationships and interactions. That early work opened so many possibilities for me that I decided to dedicate my career to applied research and practice focused on leadership effectiveness, workforce performance, and organizational transformation. Over the past twenty-five years, I have, alongside my colleagues, built upon and expanded my dissertation, which led to development of the LEAP model.

PERSONAL MASTERY

People who demonstrate personal mastery know their strengths yet also look constantly for opportunities to improve themselves. Three essential ingredients of personal improvement are commitment, curiosity, and courage.

Personal mastery includes the ability to be curious, to want to learn new things. It means staying focused (even when everyday life derails concentration) on one's personal mission and vision and being prepared for potential upsets and pitfalls. With personal mastery, we expand our individual results through commitment, curiosity, and courage.

Many work environments can stifle curiosity. But we're all born curious! I suggest cultivating curiosity, because if we're not being curious, we're not stretching our brains and finding new and better ways of doing things. The kind of courage needed from leaders in the workplace is to take risks, step outside of comfort zones, learn from failure, and, ultimately (as we'll soon see), learn to dribble the ball with both hands. What happens when we try new things? A lot of times, we don't succeed. I heard an example once about learning to play basketball. If a team member can only dribble with the right hand, even if he or she is great at it, what's the coach going to require right away? Dribbling with the left hand! How do we feel when we start dribbling with our left hand when we don't know how? It's ugly; we lose the ball. Why is the coach insisting that we do that even though it's not pretty? She doesn't want us to have the ball taken away when everybody figures out that we can only dribble with our right hand. As a one-handed dribbler, we're a risk to the team.

If we want to improve, we must be committed, first and foremost, to our own personal well-being and growth as a person.

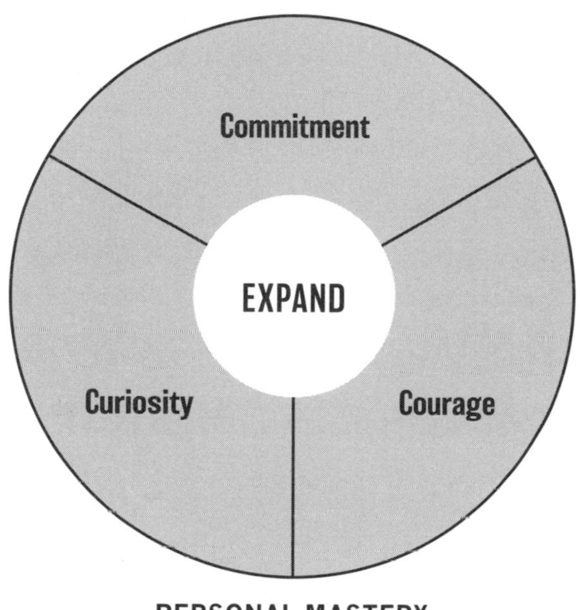

PERSONAL MASTERY

When I was a child working many weekends and summers on my family farm, growing tobacco in addition to the staple crops we ate, I could have easily grown resentful. But my parents never complained and always maintained their commitment. They taught me that no matter what we're producing, whether it's vegetables, cars, or computer chips, focusing on goals and working to expand our abilities makes the difference.

Working on the farm with my family as a child and watching my dad do the same and then return to Morristown during the week to his job as a foreman in a furniture factory taught me a lot. In particular, it taught me the value of unbending purpose. Every task and challenge my dad undertook linked to the ultimate goal of keeping our family out of debt, buying a home, and ensuring a solid future for his children. Without knowing it as such, my dad was personally masterful, and he served as a role model for me, my brothers, and for many others.

INTERPERSONAL MASTERY

People with strong interpersonal mastery understand people. They choose an optimistic attitude, listen well, look for and hear solutions to problems, and seize opportunities for bringing everyone to the table.

Interpersonally masterful people exhibit the capacity to get along with others while getting the job done. They connect, communicate, and collaborate.

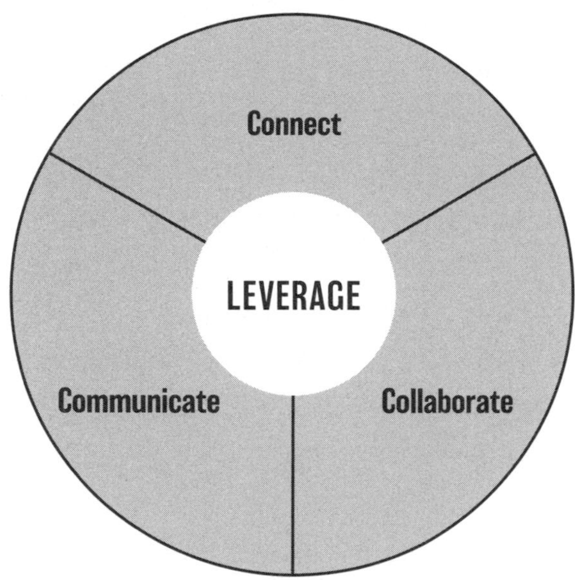

INTERPERSONAL MASTERY

When I was a child, as a family, we would get downhearted sometimes. We faced many obstacles. But my dad was always so good at helping us stay connected. He taught me that a group of people with one mind and one mission who really care about one another can achieve great things.

At one point, the workers at my dad's factory went on strike to oppose unsafe working conditions. Even though my dad was a foreman, he joined the workers he supervised on the picket line as an act of solidarity. When things didn't work out and the strike failed, he endured the same fate alongside the men and women he oversaw—he lost his job.

But those workers didn't forget my dad's commitment to connecting and collaborating with the people he managed. When he started his own catering business and owned a food truck that brought meals to several locations, those same people (who ended up working at other factories) purchased his soups, sandwiches, and snacks. They appreciated his kindness, integrity, dependability, stories, and jokes. Many of them even attended his funeral years later. His ability to connect with others was magical.

My father's example emphasizes another point I made earlier, that the masteries are interconnected; my dad's commitment to work and family extended to the way he approached those who worked for him. His ability to connect proved inspirational, motivating them not just at work, but years later in their willingness to support his business.

ORGANIZATIONAL MASTERY

People who possess organizational mastery exhibit an understanding of systems and how all the elements of the system work together in an enterprise. They also have a solid grasp of the value chain: people, processes, inputs, suppliers, outputs, customers, and outcomes. They are total-systems thinkers.

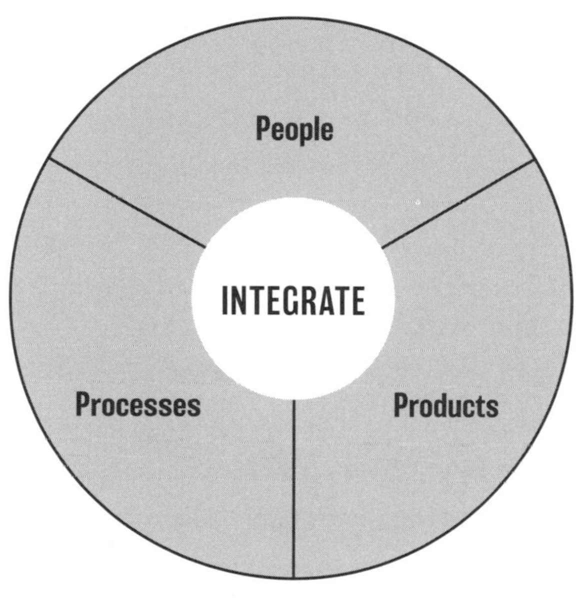

ORGANIZATIONAL MASTERY

Ed Catmull, president of Pixar Animation Studios and Walt Disney Animation Studios, demonstrates his understanding of organizational mastery in a creative way consistent with the enterprise he leads. He writes:

> People tend to think of creativity as a mysterious solo act, and they typically reduce products to a single idea: This is a movie about toys, or dinosaurs, or love, they'll say. However, in filmmaking and many other kinds of complex product development, creativity involves a large number of people from different disciplines working effectively together to solve a great many problems. The initial idea for the movie—what people in the movie business call "the high concept"—is merely one step in a long, arduous process that takes four to five years.[1]

Whether you're making sandwiches or movies, the concept he speaks to is an essential realization about organizational mastery.

After my dad launched his catering business, I had the opportunity to see firsthand just how organizationally masterful he was. Maybe it was from working as a foreman at a factory and keeping track of many moving parts and people. Maybe it was managing that factory job during the week, overseeing farmwork on the weekends, and still giving time and attention to his family. Whatever it was, my dad was always situationally aware.

He could have fifty people clamoring around his food truck at lunchtime. One person would take something off the truck without paying, and he would notice it despite the chaos. Then, instead of calling people out publicly, he'd approach them privately the next day and ask if they were facing hardships that prevented them from being able to pay for their food. He saw the bigger picture of people's lives and what motivated them.

When I go into corporate or agency situations now and hear staff talking about how dire a particular situation is, I remember my dad. No matter where you go, you will find people who are overwhelmed by all the negative elements of their situation and they feel stuck. But it doesn't have to be that way. Good leadership can not only help people feel valued, but it also can paint the larger picture they are all working toward and help them see their relationship to others around them.

NO MATTER WHERE YOU GO, YOU WILL FIND PEOPLE WHO ARE OVERWHELMED BY ALL THE NEGATIVE ELEMENTS OF THEIR SITUATION AND THEY FEEL STUCK. BUT IT DOESN'T HAVE TO BE THAT WAY.

MOTIVATIONAL MASTERY

People who exhibit motivational mastery inspire others. They create an environment where everyone wants to perform at their best. This results in sustainable achievement of individual and organizational goals. Those with motivational mastery engage, elevate, and energize.

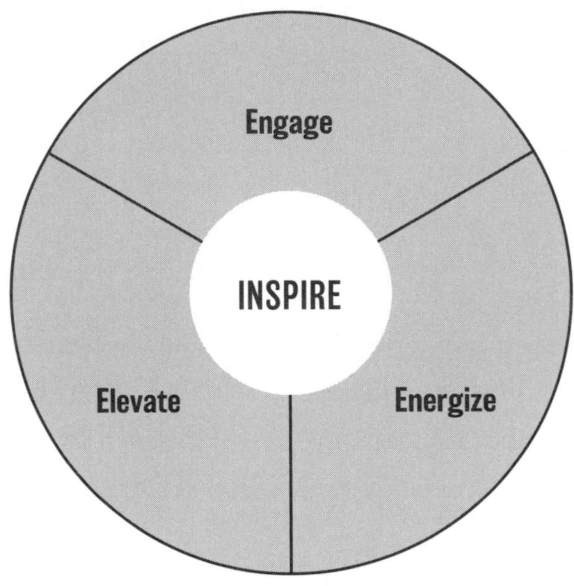

MOTIVATIONAL MASTERY

When I think about my dad and all the cares and responsibilities he had weighing on him, I'm amazed at how readily he held our family together and inspired us. He kept all of us energized and happy with love and optimism. And because of that, we achieved our family dreams; we bought that home when I was thirteen, my dad launched his own business (which he later sold to fund his retirement), and my brothers and I successfully pursued higher education. He helped us do all that by being motivationally masterful.

My dad understood a principle that the most successful people understand: setbacks and challenges can fuel increased determination and motivation. Venus Williams, one of the all-time greats of tennis, said it eloquently:

> Losses have propelled me to even bigger places, so I understand the importance of losing. You can never get complacent because a loss is always around the corner. It's in any game that you're in—a business game or whatever—you can't get complacent.[2]

MASTERY IN ACTION:

Teresa Carlson, Superhero in Motion

Over the course of my years working with leaders, I've met many inspiring people. Few better exemplify personal, interpersonal, organizational, and motivational mastery than Teresa Carlson, the vice president for Amazon Web Services world wide public sector. Teresa is, in my opinion, a superhero who is continuously expanding her own potential and effectiveness. Teresa is responsible for strategy, operations, and growth for Amazon's Web Services and Cloud Computing business. She drives both revenue and partnership strategy across the public sector and serves as Amazon's lead public-policy advisor for the global public sector.

As if her work demands weren't enough, Teresa also serves in philanthropic and leadership roles to support her community, including board chair of the American Red Cross in the national capital region, member of the American Red Cross Tiffany Circle national philanthropic committee, the Northern Virginia Technology Council board, The Women's Center board, vice chair of the public sector board of TechAmerica, the USO of Metropolitan Washington board, and The Wolf Trap Foundation board.

I've known Teresa for close to a decade, serving with her for seven of those years on the Northern Virginia Technology Council board and the American Red Cross Tiffany Circle. Teresa serves as a role model for me as a leader of leaders on many fronts. I consider her to be a stellar example of someone who is personally, interpersonally, organizationally, and motivationally masterful.

In terms of personal mastery, Teresa knows what she believes is important and courageously takes on leadership roles in causes that are aligned with her values. With respect to taking care of herself, she makes healthy choices and makes time to exercise, even when she's tired. She is curious and continues to seize opportunities to grow long after graduating with an MS degree in communications and speech and language pathology. Watching her energy and commitment to lifelong learning is inspiring.

Even though she is constantly traveling around the globe, Teresa finds a way to make time for others, consistently demonstrating the tenets of interpersonal mastery. For example, a few months ago, I needed advice regarding a board leadership issue that I was struggling with in my role as board chair of a nonprofit organization. Despite her demanding schedule, she responded immediately from halfway around the world. During our phone conversation, she offered the wisdom, support, guidance, and ideas that I was seeking. I was touched, grateful, and impressed that she would make the time for me. I've heard from many others that she has done the same for them.

Teresa is organizationally masterful. Not only do clients and colleagues like Teresa, they respect her commitment to people, processes, products, and performance. If you read about her, you'll discover that over the past twenty years she has driven innovation and change and produced successful business results time and time again. She is a highly respected leader, and her customer focus has delivered exceptional value to her clients while consistently exceeding her organization's business goals. As evidence of her total-systems leadership approach, she has received many awards, such as the FCW Federal 100 Eagle Award for her service to the federal government customer, and was one of *Washingto-*

nian magazine's "100 Most Powerful Women." She was also named to *FAST Company*'s list of the twelve top executives in its most influential women in technology category. These are just a few of numerous awards that recognize her mastery of complex systems and her ability to innovate.

Prior to her work at Amazon, Teresa led numerous transformations that required motivational prowess, including leadership positions at Microsoft and Lexign and fifteen years in the health care field. Part of her motivational magic as a rising leader over the years is that she cares about people, and it shows. Teresa engages, elevates, and energizes people wherever she goes. For example, in April of 2018, I sat with her at a Northern Virginia Technology Council Titans Breakfast at the Ritz Carlton. She was about to speak to an audience of over five hundred people, and she had just arrived that morning in Virginia on an international flight. Not only was she the life of our table, she took time to congratulate my colleague, Janelle Millard, and me on the recent launch of our new LEAP app. When she took the stage, Teresa mentioned the app to the crowd as a way of helping bring visibility to our new tool for leaders. Of course, Teresa didn't have to make the effort to mention our new app to that room full of executives, but that is just the kind of person she is.

Recently, I attended a private gathering of industry

leaders where Teresa spoke about what it would mean for the Northern Virginia and DC area now that Amazon is building out a headquarters in Arlington. The meeting was enlightening and what stuck out to me the most was hearing Teresa speak of her commitment to inclusion, involvement, and engagement as part of Amazon's expansion. It was apparent to me that her passion for fairness and diversity touched the hearts and minds of every executive in that room. My take on Teresa is that she continuously finds ways to unleash her superpowers to make a difference in the world. She is a true role model.

BRINGING IT ALL TOGETHER

Leadership effectiveness includes managing our preferences, our impulses, and our goals. It requires conscious living and knowing who we are. It demands managing our commitment, curiosity, and courage in order to live life to its fullest. Effective leaders are masterful.

Being personally, interpersonally, organizationally, and motivationally masterful sets transformational leaders apart. They are more alive, awake, and alert, reflecting a heightened state of consciousness. It's in that state where our growth occurs.

Questions for Reflection, Discovery, and Action

1. What would happen if I exhibited more commitment, curiosity, and courage in my daily activities?
2. How would my relationships improve if I were better at connecting, communicating, and collaborating?
3. Why is it important for me to know something about the people, processes, and products that are part of my organization?
4. Who would be happier if I consistently behaved in ways that engaged, elevated, and energized others?
5. If I were to suddenly become more personally, interpersonally, organizationally, and motivationally masterful, what would others see me doing that they don't see me doing now?

3

DISCOVER YOUR SUPERPOWERS

To better understand human behavior and leadership effectiveness, I spent several years of my early career conducting research and gathering data. For example, I ran scores of controlled lab experiments on leader emergence. In addition, I spent many months studying how different factors affect managers' ratings of others' work performance. I also observed hundreds of supervisors and their subordinates in manufacturing settings. My desire to figure out what makes people successful was very strong. Perhaps part of the passion I developed for understanding what drives success, satisfaction, and motivation came from my experience watching my dad. But what my parents taught me, like what those years of careful observation and research taught me, was that transformational leadership ultimately happens when people become personally, interpersonally, organizationally, and motivationally masterful.

I also saw such mastery in action among my TSI team members and a vast number of Department of Defense (DoD) leaders and employees over a decade ago when our country had a critical, immediate, and time-sensitive mission to save lives.

The essential job at hand was speeding up a DoD program's ability to build, deliver, and repair military vehicles that protected men and women on the ground in Iraq and Afghanistan from death and dismemberment from mines and improvised explosive devices (IEDs). It was a threat they faced every day in the field.

Motivation is clear in an instance like this when people's lives are at stake. And the DoD program accomplished its mission with a speed of implementation not seen since World War II, fielding and quickly repairing vehicles to protect the lives of those who were protecting our country. It was an instance where the TSI team helped leaders boost their effectiveness in a very short amount of time. And it was a client engagement that helped me more clearly define and develop the LEAP Profile. You can probably imagine both the urgency and the responsibility we all felt given what was at stake. It was the sort of mission where we could not fail, for to do so would jeopardize warfighters' lives. I felt hard-pressed to put the observation and research I'd been doing in earlier parts of my career into action. We were all asked to complete a daunting mission, to say the least. The DoD is a large enterprise with complex processes and layered bureaucracies. In order to pull off the speed of implementation required for success, we would have to live by the four masteries of LEAP and, equally important, apply them in integrative ways to help transform the entire system.

This chapter will build on the four masteries introduced earlier and introduce three areas of acumen essential to each. From there, the book will take a deep dive into each mastery in its rightful order. Because of the overview provided here, this is a good chapter to mark for return reference later—or to have open in front of you when first using the LEAP app or completing the LEAP Profile.

HOW TO USE THE LEAP PROFILE

The LEAP Profile is based on evidence showing that individuals with strong personal, interpersonal, organizational, and motivational mastery tend to become superheroes among those they lead. Leaders who maximize their superpowers soar to the leading edge of performance. Individuals who do not develop in these areas can easily stall out.

Becoming more masterful will have a direct impact on those you lead. Research from Dale Carnegie reveals that companies with engaged employees outperform those without by up to 202 percent.[1] And according to the *Harvard Business Review,* happy employees have an average of 31 percent higher productivity, 37 percent higher sales, and three times greater creativity.[2] Transformational leaders attract and influence people, because these leaders understand how to lift communication, relationships, and motivation to new heights.

The LEAP Profile is a powerful tool that can help you make decisions about your self-development and begin your transformation to be at the leading edge of performance. Whether you are just starting your career, thinking about a professional change, or propelling yourself toward even greater results in your current role, you can benefit from the wealth of information reflected in your LEAP Profile. To download the LEAP app and complete the profile, visit TheLEAPapp.com. The LEAP Profile questions are also included in this chapter.

As you complete your profile, remember that managing self-development is not a one-time event but a series of decisions made over your lifetime. By understanding where you currently stand with your mastery in all four areas, you will be able to better target your development in the areas that are most useful to you. Once you have downloaded the LEAP app and completed your LEAP Profile, you'll have a snapshot of where you are now and what you need to do to develop further in any of the four leadership masteries. Or, if you prefer, you can use the profile questions provided here to assess yourself.

LEADERSHIP EFFECTIVENESS AND POTENTIAL (LEAP) PROFILE

For each item below, please circle how you rate yourself on a scale ranging from low to high.

Personal: I seize opportunities to improve myself.

LOW	LOW-MEDIUM	MEDIUM	MEDIUM-HIGH	HIGH

Commitment: I am clear about what I value.

LOW	LOW-MEDIUM	MEDIUM	MEDIUM-HIGH	HIGH

Curiosity: I seek to learn new things.

LOW	LOW-MEDIUM	MEDIUM	MEDIUM-HIGH	HIGH

Courage: I choose to step out of my comfort zone.

LOW	LOW-MEDIUM	MEDIUM	MEDIUM-HIGH	HIGH

Interpersonal: I leverage relationships.

LOW	LOW-MEDIUM	MEDIUM	MEDIUM-HIGH	HIGH

Connect: I establish strong bonds with others.

LOW	LOW-MEDIUM	MEDIUM	MEDIUM-HIGH	HIGH

Communicate: I effectively exchange information with others.

LOW	LOW-MEDIUM	MEDIUM	MEDIUM-HIGH	HIGH

Collaborate: I work with others to create greater impact than working alone.

LOW	LOW-MEDIUM	MEDIUM	MEDIUM-HIGH	HIGH

Organizational: I recognize how people, processes, and products create success in my workplace.

LOW	LOW-MEDIUM	MEDIUM	MEDIUM-HIGH	HIGH

People: I understand the roles of others in my organization.

LOW	LOW-MEDIUM	MEDIUM	MEDIUM-HIGH	HIGH

Processes: I comprehend the flow of work in my organization.

LOW	LOW-MEDIUM	MEDIUM	MEDIUM-HIGH	HIGH

Products: I know what my organization provides to customers.

LOW	LOW-MEDIUM	MEDIUM	MEDIUM-HIGH	HIGH

Motivational: I inspire others to perform with excellence.

LOW	LOW-MEDIUM	MEDIUM	MEDIUM-HIGH	HIGH

Engage: I find ways to include and involve others.

LOW	LOW-MEDIUM	MEDIUM	MEDIUM-HIGH	HIGH

Elevate: I actively lift up my coworkers to support their well-being.

LOW	LOW-MEDIUM	MEDIUM	MEDIUM-HIGH	HIGH

Energize: I boost the morale of others.

LOW	LOW-MEDIUM	MEDIUM	MEDIUM-HIGH	HIGH

PERSONAL MASTERY: BUILDING YOUR BEST SELF

Personal mastery is the ability to know one's strengths while leveraging opportunities for improvement. It also includes the ability to hold a proper attitude for learning new things. Personally masterful people are self-aware; they seek out and act on feedback.

Personally masterful people see their connections to everything around them. They maintain focus on their personal mission and vision even when things go wrong. Personally masterful leaders expand their results with commitment, curiosity, and courage.

Once you've completed your LEAP Profile, you'll have taken a look at your own current strengths and opportunities for growth. Your profile results will summarize your self-assessment of each area:

- **COMMITMENT**: Do you proactively honor your mind, body, spirit, and values? People who score high in this component take action to make their overall well-being a priority. People who score low in this component do not prioritize their well-being and may get off track with their goals, health, and values.
- **CURIOSITY**: Do you seek to expand your knowledge and insight? People who score high in this component embrace formal and informal opportunities to learn

and grow. People who score low in this component ask fewer questions, avoid trying new things, and are less likely to enroll in nonrequisite training.

- **COURAGE:** Are you willing to step out of your comfort zone? People who score high in this component seek out ways to challenge themselves and learn from their failures. People who score low in this component avoid taking risks and are less resilient in the face of setbacks.

INTERPERSONAL MASTERY: MAKING RELATIONSHIPS MATTER

Interpersonal mastery is the ability to get along with others and leverage everyone's talents to get the job done. It includes skill in communication, listening, and fostering a positive attitude. Interpersonally masterful people make connections with their coworkers and respect the contributions of others. They are more productive because of their propensity to project optimism, look for solutions to problems, and seize opportunities to create new alliances. They also focus on successfully leveraging relationships through connections, communication, and collaboration.

Your LEAP Profile will help you assess your own interpersonal mastery in the following areas:

- **CONNECTION**: Do you build and leverage relationships by getting along with others while maintaining focus on getting the job done? Interpersonally masterful people seek true connections with colleagues and respect the contributions of others. Those who score low on the connection component prefer working by themselves and don't seek out the strengths and contributions of others.
- **COMMUNICATION**: Do you work to establish strong bonds, goodwill, and common ground with people? Do you effectively gather and share information with colleagues both in person and in writing? People who score high in this component create a welcoming environment where people feel comfortable sharing opinions and concerns. Those who score low in this component unintentionally alienate others by failing to express interest in them.
- **COLLABORATION**: Do you demonstrate that teamwork can create greater impacts and stronger results than working alone? People who score high in collaboration tend to seek out new teaming opportunities, take interest in others' opinions, and provide prompt and thoughtful feedback. They get more done and excel in teams and group environments. Those who score low in this component tend to find themselves revising their own work or that of others. They may

also feel they have less control over results and may believe teamwork is a waste of time.

ORGANIZATIONAL MASTERY: PUTTING ALL THE PIECES TOGETHER

Organizational mastery involves understanding how decisions and policies influence one another across an organization. Organizationally masterful people consider the effect decisions will have across the organization and what long-term impacts will occur as a result of those decisions. The organization can be your workplace, your place of worship, an association you belong to, a charity you support, etc. In organizations, systems consist of people, processes, and products that work together to make an enterprise sustainable and successful. Organizationally masterful people understand how all elements must be integrated in the environment to achieve desired outcomes.

Your LEAP Profile can tell you a lot about your level of organizational mastery by helping you evaluate yourself in the following areas:

- **PEOPLE**: Do you understand, support, and leverage the various roles individuals play throughout the organization? Organizationally masterful people consider the impact different roles can have across the organization and what long-term effects may result. They also seek ways to align themselves and others with the vision of the organization and seek a purpose for their actions. Those who are low in organizational mastery tend to solve immediate problems without examining how the solution will affect people and products across the organization and over time. Low scorers may also align themselves and others to do exactly as instructed without considering other possibilities for reaching goals.

- **PROCESSES**: Do you understand the actions and steps required to support overall organizational goals? Those who score high in organizational mastery operate with a focus on how different actions and steps fit into the whole and could establish lasting change in their organization. People who score low in this component may not appreciate the impact of processes on the larger enterprise and may communicate less as process changes occur.
- **PRODUCTS**: Do you focus on creating excellent outputs and stellar products that delight customers? Organizationally masterful individuals tend to be high performers and develop exceptional work products. People who score low in this component settle for acceptable performance and often strive for no more than adequate work products.

MOTIVATIONAL MASTERY: INSPIRING EVERYONE AROUND YOU

To excel in any aspect of life requires motivation, something that is both internally and externally driven. Individuals with motivational mastery understand how to maintain their own motivation and help others manifest it. They support sustainable achievement of individual and organizational goals.

INDIVIDUALS WITH MOTIVATIONAL MASTERY UNDERSTAND HOW TO MAINTAIN THEIR OWN MOTIVATION AND HELP OTHERS MANIFEST IT.

By attending to motivation, masterful leaders are better able to mentor and accelerate people's professional development and alignment within the organization. Motivational mastery focuses on inspiring performance as you engage, elevate, and energize yourself and others.

Motivational mastery requires acumen in the following three areas:

- **ENGAGEMENT**: Do you include and involve everyone in supporting achievement of individual and enterprise goals? Do you boost morale, satisfaction, and happiness in those around you? People who exhibit high motivational mastery align others toward goals and inspire their best efforts. When motivational masters are gone, their absence is felt by the whole team. People who are low in this skill find that others are moving in different directions and not coming together to create results. They also may frequently engage in negative discussions about work or others.

- **ELEVATION**: Do you bring out the best in others and actively lift up your colleagues to support their development? People who score high in this component provide encouraging feedback and recognition to those around them. They also operate with the intention of brightening people's days. People who score low in this component tend to discourage others from seeking developmental opportunities.
- **ENERGY**: Do you exhibit a positive attitude even when the going gets tough? Do you strengthen bonds among people and help them connect to and support the enterprise mission, vision, and goals? People who score high in this category strive to provide clarity and structure in the work environment, shaping workforce goals to drive organizational results. People who score low in this component tend to struggle with taking responsibility for being a source of energy in their environment.

Questions for Reflection, Discovery, and Action

1. In what areas of personal mastery am I strongest? How do I demonstrate it in everyday life? In what areas of personal mastery do I still need to grow? What actions am I open to taking this week to become more personally masterful?
2. Where do I excel with respect to interpersonal mastery? What changes am I willing to make to foster that improvement? What actions can I take today?
3. When it comes to organizational mastery, are there areas where I demonstrate particular skills and knowledge? If so, how? What areas of my organization's inner workings do I still need to understand more fully? How can I start increasing my understanding this month? What am I willing to do to build that understanding as my organization changes and grows?
4. What are my strengths when it comes to motivational mastery? Where do I still need to improve? What actions could I start implementing now to inspire people who are within my sphere of influence?
5. When it comes to demonstrating personal, interpersonal, organizational, and motivational mastery, what prevents me from revealing my superpowers? What is my kryptonite?

4

EXPAND YOUR PERSONAL MASTERY

When TSI was supporting the ten-year DoD effort I mentioned in the previous chapter, helping them more efficiently supply mission-critical and life-saving equipment to our troops, one of our most pressing concerns was that the people stateside working to help the troops abroad were also taking care of *themselves*.

Unsurprisingly, given the accelerated time line of the mission and the fact that all of these DoD employees and contractors were committed to saving lives, many of our clients were not getting enough sleep. They would frequently stay at the office all night and not go home from work. In response, there were times when some of the TSI team would camp out from four o'clock in the morning until midnight, trying to help these clients manage their stress *and* their passionate commitment to the mission. It was high-visibility work as well, with status briefings being shared with White House staff and the upper echelons of the Pentagon.

We suggested to our clients that, yes, the mission is critical, but you have to preserve yourself to perform the mission well. It all goes back to that airline-safety directive to put the oxygen mask on yourself before you help other people. We considered it part of *our* mission to remind our clients to take Saturday off or go on a walk and relax for thirty minutes.

I urge you to extend the same courtesy to yourself that we encouraged those clients to give themselves. Whatever your role is, whatever your latest mission, you cannot perform at your highest levels if you're not attending to your mind, body, and spirit.

People who are personally masterful understand this and manage their minds, bodies, and spirits the same way they manage their various roles at the office or in the field. They take responsibility for the results they achieve, and they hold a proper attitude for learning new things. They see their connection to everything around them, whether a situation is going well or not. They remain focused and prepared for every life event.

Personally masterful people inspire change, welcome change, foster change, and sustain change. They're also willing to change themselves. Success relies on practicing personal mastery—not as if it were a one-hour commitment to take a Pilates class or to meditate occasionally but as a choice to evolve every day toward higher levels of ability and effectiveness. For our DoD clients, that meant being committed to self-care as well as the care of our troops overseas.

PERSONALLY MASTERFUL PEOPLE INSPIRE CHANGE, WELCOME CHANGE, FOSTER CHANGE, AND SUSTAIN CHANGE. THEY'RE ALSO WILLING TO CHANGE THEMSELVES.

People who advance to the leading edge of performance have personal mastery. They continuously work to expand and leverage their effectiveness when it comes to commitment, curiosity, and courage. Throughout this chapter I will dive into these three essential elements of personal mastery and share some concrete means to help you evolve into your most committed, curious, and courageous self.

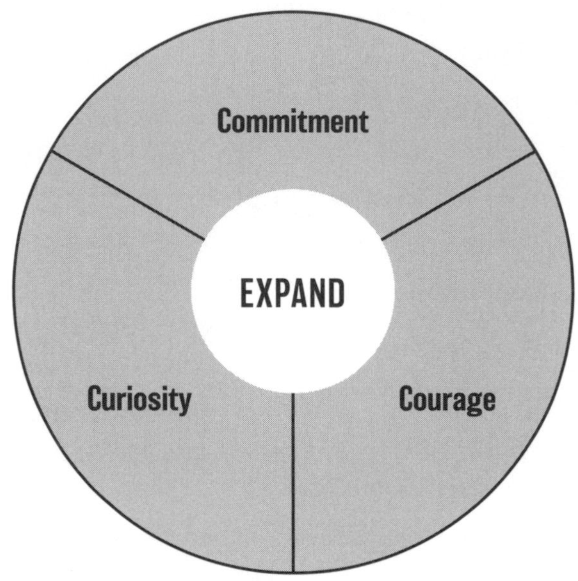

COMMITMENT: HOW TO GROW IT

A leader's commitments shape his or her organization's identity, define its strengths and weaknesses, establish its opportunities and limitations, and set its direction. Commitments enable as well as constrain and provide continuity over time. "Despite differences in their personal attributes, successful managers all excel in the making, honoring, and remaking of commitments."[1]

Too often in the workplace, we give all of the logical reasons why people should be committed to a given course of action, but intellectual commitment isn't enough. Our DoD clients demonstrated that clearly.

They were *emotionally* committed to helping service members in the field (and the families waiting for them to come home). We are not totally committed until we are emotionally committed, too.

Leaders pave the way for people to become more emotionally committed to the mission at hand. That's easier said than done, of course. We're not all on lifesaving missions where emotional engagement is natural. So how do we cultivate both intellectual and emotional engagement within ourselves and others? Personal mastery enables us to make conscious choices to evolve and embrace change. We become freer to respond with clarity, commitment, and energy, regardless of the circumstances around us. Here are two actions you can take to strengthen commitment:

1. **BE INTENTIONAL.** Be clear about your goals, professional and personal, and make sure your daily actions reflect your commitment to those goals. Most of us are pretty clear on what we don't want. Can you be as clear about what you *do* want? For example, if you want to be healthier and devote more time to exercise, then be intentional; set your alarm thirty minutes earlier three times a week and go for a morning walk, or hit the gym on the way to the office. When you are at work, continue this intentional pattern; write down commitments you make

in meetings, and build daily, weekly, or monthly intention check-in time into your calendar.

2. **HONOR YOUR VALUES.** It's much easier to commit to something that is valuable to you. Think about what your values are, and then make sure your goals at work and at home align with them. For example, if you're in a company whose products harm the environment, and you're passionate about protecting the earth, understand that you're never going to be able to truly commit yourself to that job. Make sure the role you occupy and the mission you have are aligned with your values, and if they're not, start drafting a game plan for how to change that. And don't forget, honoring your values helps build trust in others.

MAKE SURE THE ROLE YOU OCCUPY AND THE MISSION YOU HAVE ARE ALIGNED WITH YOUR VALUES, AND IF THEY'RE NOT, START DRAFTING A GAME PLAN FOR HOW TO CHANGE THAT.

THROUGH THE LENS OF SCIENCE:
Emotional Intelligence

Emotional intelligence (EQ) is our ability to identify and manage our own emotions, as well as our ability to recognize and help manage the emotions of others. Emotional intelligence includes (1) perception of emotions, (2) using emotions to guide thought, (3) understanding emotions, and (4) managing emotions. Emotional intelligence is linked to increased job performance and job satisfaction. It is also linked to lower rates of job burnout.

Transformational leaders exhibit high emotional intelligence. They hone their ability to recognize and acknowledge their own and others' feelings. They respect the role that emotions play in behavior and use their understanding of their own and others' emotions to guide their perceptions and subsequent actions.

In an analysis of competency models from 188 companies, the majority of which were large global corporations, the ratio of technical skills, IQ, and EQ were measured, and the results showed that emotional intelligence was viewed as twice as important as other skills for jobs at all levels. The analysis also showed that among senior positions, nearly 90 percent of success was attributed to emotional intelligence.

Leaders with high EQ practice self-awareness and regulation. Leaders who are high in EQ are less likely to experience the negative effects of stress, because they can recognize signs of stress earlier and are better equipped to identify and utilize healthy coping mechanisms.[2]

CURIOSITY: HOW TO CULTIVATE IT

Curiosity and open-mindedness are critical traits for transformational leaders. They help leaders expand their perspective and find success, even in challenging times. Curiosity is about seeking fresh ideas and approaches in order to keep pace with change. Real leadership guided by curiosity "may be less about having all the answers and more about wondering and questioning."[3]

Curiosity is so important it holds a place as one of the three key psychological qualities that enhance our ability to manage complexity: Intelligence Quotient (IQ), Emotional Quotient (EQ), and Curiosity Quotient (CQ). People who rank high in CQ are inquisitive, open to new experiences, find novelty exciting, and tend to generate many original ideas. "Individuals with higher CQ are generally more tolerant of ambiguity. This nuanced, sophisticated, subtle thinking style defines the very essence of complexity."[4]

Yet sadly, curiosity is underappreciated and underemphasized despite research that shows curiosity and motivation to learn are significant contributors to achievement. "Having a 'hungry mind' is a core determinant of academic achievement, rivaling the prediction power of IQ."[5]

Do you need to cultivate more curiosity in your life? Here are two key actions you can take to develop a more curious attitude:

1. **SEEK EDUCATION.** Learning doesn't have to take place in a formal training program. The idea is to build your knowledge base and reignite your innate desire to explore. If you feel like your management style just isn't working, read a book (like this one!) once a week that will help you explore new ways of leading your team.
2. **ASK QUESTIONS.** You don't have all the answers. No one does. Acknowledge that, and start asking questions of your employees, other managers, your friends, maybe even that smiling person in the grocery store line. Everyone has expertise in something. Find out what other people know, collect new perspectives, and watch the magic that happens—new ideas will start coming to you much more quickly.

YOU DON'T HAVE ALL THE ANSWERS. NO ONE DOES. ACKNOWLEDGE THAT, AND START ASKING QUESTIONS.

COURAGE: HOW TO EXPAND YOURS

In *The Wizard of Oz*, the cowardly lion had courage all along. In the end, he unleashed it. Courageous leaders take risks and make decisions with the intention of launching change in their industries. Their boldness inspires their teams, energizes customers, and positions their organizations for transformational success. "Courage is the quality that distinguishes great leaders from excellent managers."[6]

What does courage look like? It's about taking a stand, making a move, and pushing through fear. Courage isn't absence of fear; it's refusing to let fear hold you back. As Ben Dean writes: "If any virtues are to be cultivated within a society, one might reasonably argue that courage should be foremost among them, for courage may be necessary to maintaining and exercising the other virtues."[7]

Malala Yousafzai grew up in Pakistan at a time when the Pakistani Taliban began imposing strict Islamic law, destroying or shutting down girls' schools and banning women from playing an active role in society. As a young girl, Malala actively went against the Taliban and demanded that girls be allowed to receive an education. As a result of her activist efforts, she was shot by a Taliban gunman in 2012 at the age of fifteen but survived and went on to receive the Nobel Peace Prize. Malala said of her activist efforts, "We were scared, but our fear was not as strong as our courage."[8]

There are many different types of courage, including (1) feeling fear yet choosing to act, (2) following your heart, (3) persevering in the face of adversity, (4) standing up for what is right, (5) expanding your horizons and letting go of the familiar, and (6) facing suffering with dignity or faith. "From the Bible to fairy tales; ancient myths to Hollywood movies, our culture is rich with exemplary tales of bravery and self-sacrifice for the greater good."[9]

HUMANS AREN'T BORN COURAGEOUS. IT'S A TRAIT WE CHOOSE AND THEN CULTIVATE.

Humans aren't born courageous. It's a trait we choose and then cultivate. If you want to practice more courage in your life and profession, try these ideas:

1. **STEP OUT OF YOUR COMFORT ZONE.** Humans have evolved to develop habits. It makes us more efficient if we don't have to think about everything we do, like brushing our teeth every night before bed or driving the same route to work every morning. Habits aren't always bad, but when it comes to being a more effective person—figuring out better ways to meet our goals or creating a new product—we have to leave old habits behind and be open to trying something new. This also helps us keep our mental powers nimble. You can easily try stepping out of your comfort zone today. Something as simple as moving your watch from your left to your right wrist will get your brain connecting new synapses. Go further: ask a colleague

what he thinks of an idea you've felt anxious about sharing with the whole team, or take a training course in some area of your business that has never been your strength, be it marketing through social media or honing public speaking skills.

2. **WELCOME CHANGE.** It's human nature to fear change. And fear isn't necessarily a bad thing—it can help us exercise due caution in challenging circumstances. But even if you feel apprehensive about change, work on welcoming it for the lessons and innovations it often provides. And don't stop at getting comfortable with change; start fostering it, too! People and companies that can't embrace and adjust to change go the way of Blockbuster Video. Will you be nimble enough to navigate a major market shift in the future? Start practicing for it. For example, adopt that new customer-relationship management system everyone says the organization needs to increase efficiencies, but which you dread implementing because it will result in a whole new set of processes, technology skills, and training. Or apply for that position in a field that's entirely new to you,

PEOPLE AND COMPANIES THAT CAN'T EMBRACE AND ADJUST TO CHANGE GO THE WAY OF BLOCKBUSTER VIDEO.

but where you feel you could bring critical skills to bear. Once you start seeing change as an opportunity for growth, your capacity to embrace it (and roll with it) will grow.

The process of personal mastery forces us to do what most people have a very hard time doing—assessing ourselves as more than the sum of a list of faults. As our focus broadens, so too does the accuracy of our self-assessment. In addition to our talents and strengths, we begin to identify opportunities for growth. But in the context of personal mastery, some weaknesses turn out to be nothing more than strengths that have not been fully developed. The question is not how to get rid of them, but how to harness their full power. The common excuse for avoiding change—I *can't* do it!—is replaced by something more honest and more possible. Transformation becomes the imperative.

It's within your power to shift your energy and become more personally masterful. Here are some additional action items to try:

- **BE AUTHENTICALLY AND COURAGEOUSLY YOURSELF.** It doesn't matter if you're not competent at everything. Be willing to admit that. When you rely exclusively on competence to problem-solve, you self-limit. What strengths do you currently have that can help you achieve your goals?

- **BE CURIOUS.** Try something new, even if it's something relatively simple like riding your bike the two miles to work instead of driving. What was that like? Did it change your perspective on your commute? Challenging and new activities increase your brain's elasticity *and* improve your ability to handle unfamiliar situations.

- **SET PRIORITIES THAT ALIGN WITH YOUR VALUES.** Reorganize and prioritize your work (and your life) based on what you value most. If you value quality time with your family and you're not getting enough of it, then don't be afraid to realign your work schedule to accommodate more time with the people you love. When your priorities are being met, you feel more energized to accomplish goals at work and in life and will prove more productive.

CHALLENGING AND NEW ACTIVITIES INCREASE YOUR BRAIN'S ELASTICITY AND IMPROVE YOUR ABILITY TO HANDLE UNFAMILIAR SITUATIONS.

- **FAIL WITH PURPOSE.** Recognize that failure is part of the growth and learning process. Don't avoid changing how you do things or implementing a new strategy at work because you're afraid of failure. Feel the blessing of learning from failure, and ask yourself how a particular failure has improved your understanding, motivated you to change, or offered insights on potential new methods for achieving your goals. As a caution, it's important not to risk anyone's safety or well-being when trying this.

- **COMMIT TO AND PRACTICE RESILIENCE.** Even when things don't go your way, don't let disappointment send you into a headlong plummet. Stay focused on your long-term goals. Get up, brush yourself off, and try again in a new way.
- **REMEMBER SELF-CARE.** Everything in your life will suffer if you don't take care of *yourself.* Set aside time in your day for relaxing and recharging. Your mental and physical health impacts your performance. Even taking a quick walk can give you the mental clarity you need to tackle a problem. Take time.
- **STOP PROCRASTINATING.** It's often a protective mechanism to keep you from failure, but if you don't risk and if you don't fail, you won't learn. Start small if you need to and commit to doing one small thing every day to get you closer to your goals. The important thing is to stop stalling and start moving in the direction of your dreams.

MASTERY IN ACTION:
Meryl Streep—Practice Makes Perfect

A few years ago, I had the opportunity to spend some time with Meryl Streep. At the time, I served on the advisory board of the National Women's History Museum, and Meryl agreed to emcee their awards gala that honored women in science. I had watched her movies over the years and followed her career as she became an award-winning actress.

Meryl arrived early to spend time with the attendees at the pre-reception. I was curious to meet a woman who was so successful in her profession. As I waited in line to meet her, I noticed she was calm and collected even though she was going to go on stage within the hour.

Meryl seemed relaxed and at ease, and as I watched I noticed that with every person she met, she seemed curious, open, and energetic. When it was my turn to speak with her, I enjoyed it very much!

As I walked away from Meryl, I thought, "As a CEO I don't have many mentors in my life. I could expand my definition of mentor to people who I admire, and I could be intentional about that." For the rest of the evening, I made it a point to watch Meryl ... her energy and her body language. When the pre-reception ended, she went on stage and gave a stellar performance. She was magnificent and never missed a beat.

About a month later, Meryl returned to Washington, DC, to host a private showing of the movie *Iron Lady*. By this point, I had made her my mentor. She did not know it because my study of her and her career was from a distance. With this second chance to speak with her, I was curious about how she masters accents—accents so accurate that you don't know she's acting. I asked her how she learned to develop such an acute ear and she said, "Oh, I pay attention. That's what I do. I really pay attention." I thought, "I can do that." After that, I started paying more attention to everything. I began to realize Meryl's not just gifted. She pays attention, she's a perfectionist, and she practices.

Having paid such close attention to Meryl, I've come to see that she has applied these seemingly simple approaches with such purpose and consistency that her work appears effortless. The woman behind the roles she plays is one who is in touch with her mind, body, spirit, and values. She's curious, and she's courageous.

We can all pay attention to our surroundings. We can practice our skills. We can find mentors we admire and study how they approach their lives and their careers. We can remember that even for someone as gifted as Meryl Streep, every role is new, every film requires personal growth, and every job brings new challenges. The kind of ease she demonstrates does not come without work, and she inspires me to challenge myself to soar to new heights every day.

BRINGING IT ALL TOGETHER

When we see people who have perfected a craft, my experience is that often we can be intimidated. But, we can seek them out and learn from them. We can find people around us who have achieved excellence in what they do and learn from them. It falls on us to be curious and take a step to try, without invading their space and privacy, to discover something of value we can take on for ourselves.

As we are embarking on something new and different—a new angle in our private life or some new endeavor—we can remove a lot of the intimidation by learning from people who have already achieved the success we're aiming for. Personal mastery is about commitment to our minds, our bodies, our spirits, and our values. It's about curiosity to learn something new and the courage to fall down when we try.

Questions for Reflection, Discovery, and Action

1. What is a small, but specific, thing you can do this week to strengthen your commitment to your mind, body, spirit, and values?
2. What is a longer-term and bigger-picture commitment you can make for the coming year?
3. What is one thing you can do now to start cultivating your curiosity?
4. What is one long-term, curiosity-building initiative you can take on?
5. What is one small step you can take to expand your courage?
6. What is one thing you want to do in the coming year toward reaching a long-term goal that requires courage you haven't been able to muster yet? What would you need to do to start taking action?
7. What would you do to celebrate when you've achieved your personal mastery goals?

5

AMPLIFY YOUR INTERPERSONAL MASTERY

Before my company took on the ten-year effort to help establish more efficient systems for getting lifesaving vehicles to our troops, I remember sitting on a park bench with a TSI team member, who ultimately became the project leader. We were weighing the pros and cons of taking on this enormous assignment. We knew it was a great opportunity for us, but we also knew it was fraught with risk. For example, we would have to double the size of our consulting staff. Also, with such a high-visibility and mission-critical project, there would be no room for error.

I summoned my courage and said, "Let's go for it."

But that project took a lot more than personal mastery of courage, curiosity, and commitment. It required calling on the interpersonal mastery of our TSI team, who exercised their skills in connecting, communicating, and collaborating. With advanced training and certifications to lead complex improvement projects, they worked with the various manufacturers who supplied vehicles to the military and talked with them about what might be done to streamline the production process. And when those vehicles showed up to be shipped abroad, our team helped strengthen delicate relationships with industry representatives to facilitate faster flow and better vehicle-accounting systems.

Managing those complex relationships among so many stakeholders required interpersonal mastery on a large scale. But we did it, and we helped our clients do it as well. We helped them not only acquire and field more vehicles faster but also get those vehicles quickly back into the field after they were damaged and repaired. In order to accomplish this immense task, we and our clients had to connect, communicate, and collaborate at a masterful level while leveraging relationships.

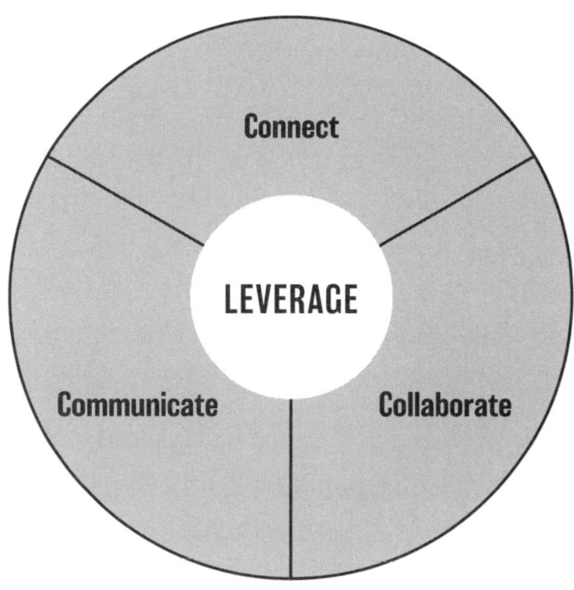

Interpersonally masterful people achieve success in challenging undertakings like this because of their propensity to project a positive attitude, listen well, look for solutions to problems, and seize opportunities for collaboration. They exhibit the capacity to get along with others while getting the job done and demonstrate they care about people. When an environment of compassion like that exists, people are much more likely to feel at ease about being a colleague, a helper, a mentor—and a leader.

Interpersonal mastery requires conscious changes in habits and attitudes when dealing with others, and it includes an ability to communicate in such a way that our new ideas can inspire people. Interpersonal mastery is also about building bonds. Strong bonds are great avenues to relay energy, vision, and impact. When we build bonds, we create more sustainable relationships. Interpersonally masterful people take it one step further, however, and nurture those bonds for the long term, because they understand the value of their relationships.

When we feel a bond with another person, it enables us to more easily overcome personal differences and avoid hard feelings. Alliances create power. Leaders seek unity in small and large, formal and informal relationships. They understand that relationships are valuable resources that contribute to achieving bold goals.

PEOPLE DO MORE WHEN THEY HAVE AUTHORITY, KNOWLEDGE, AND SUPPORT.

Empower others. People do more when they have authority, knowledge, and support. There's power in one person. We can choose to help every person to be poised to make a difference when there's a difference to be made. We can also rededicate our own talent to creating a setting where everyone is rewarded for learning, collaborating, and succeeding.

Even in the face of daunting and unpredictable conditions, we can create greater levels of possibility and performance if we master connecting, communicating, and collaborating.

CONNECT: CREATE RAPPORT WITH OTHERS

Interpersonally masterful people know how to enroll others in their goals and dreams by establishing authentic and meaningful connections with them. That means showing genuine concern and compassion for others, looking for common ground (even when you may disagree on an issue), and making relationships the core of any partnership or endeavor.

If you need to build your skills in developing connections, here are two actions you can start taking right now:

1. **INTERACT ONE-ON-ONE AND IN PERSON.** In our technology-driven world, it's easy to become physically disconnected from others, even when we may think we're staying connected because of email, texts, and social media. But nothing eclipses regular in-person interaction for building bonds and strengthening existing relationships. It's easy to hide at our desks. Instead, we can choose to devote some portion of each day to walking around and talking to our colleagues, even if it's just informal conversation. By creating one-on-one relationships, we can put others at ease and help them feel safe. It's hard to build a solid connection without trust. When we dare to be vulnerable with our family, friends, colleagues,

and employees, it lets them know we don't think we have all the answers. It shows that we care about their views and insights. And, we can honor their vulnerabilities, too, by maintaining confidentiality.

2. **SET AN EXAMPLE, AND SET THE TONE.** We can model the behaviors we expect from others. For example, if we want a work environment where failure isn't punished and risk-taking is encouraged, then we can recognize those who try new things and try new things ourselves. That also means building a supportive environment where everyone feels they're on the same team and committed to the same mission. When we model and foster a workplace that honors risk-taking and mutual support, we see more of both.

WE CAN MODEL THE VALUES WE EXPECT FROM OTHERS.

COMMUNICATE: HEAR AND BE HEARD

Communicating isn't just about getting our message across. It's also about engagement—a true conversation among family members, friends, or colleagues where everyone has a voice, is understood, and is shown that his or her contributions are valuable. How do we ensure our teammates are hearing us and that we are hearing them? How do we know if they'll actually consider what we communicate and not just interpret it as a meaningless assertion?

Clear, engaging communication means we need to do more than just give directions. It means providing a clear goal—but not over-managing how it's achieved. We can give people the freedom and authority to find their own best ways of accomplishing the mission at hand. With more autonomy, our team members will also find more meaning in their work.

Here are two tips for improving your mastery of communication:

1. **LISTEN AND LEARN.** Let people know you're curious about their ideas and open to hearing their problem-solving techniques. Listen to understand and learn. For example, if a team member has an innovative idea for increasing sales, hear him out, ask smart questions to understand him better, and think about how his ideas (or some part of them) might play into a future marketing campaign.
2. **PAY ATTENTION TO NONVERBAL COMMUNICATION.** So much of what we say is spoken by expressions, body posture, and tone of voice. Pay attention to the small cues that let you know not just that people are hearing you but that they feel you are hearing them.

THROUGH THE LENS OF SCIENCE:
Leader-Member Exchange

Leader-Member Exchange (LMX) is a leadership theory asserting that positive relationships between leaders and their subordinates contribute to improved performance on the part of employees. Simply put, employees who like their leader will perform better. Leveraging the effects of LMX is all about cultivating relationships.

Transformational leaders help people feel understood and appreciated; in turn, they show improved performance and commitment to the organization. LMX assumes that subordinates affect the relationship as more than passive recipients. LMX is grounded in the understanding that managers can develop quality relationships with their subordinates, and that they can leverage these relationships to produce improved employee performance. Through widespread, improved employee performance it can be assumed that organizational performance will also improve; both employees and the organization benefit from strong LMX.

Reported results of strong LMX include higher job performance, job satisfaction, and organizational commitment. Some of the downsides reported from weak LMX include higher turnover and role-related stress. While some leaders may find it easy, or even natural, to cultivate relationships with their employees, this can prove to be challenging for more introverted leaders. Yet research indicates that LMX is malleable and can be affected by teachable skills. To strengthen LMX, leaders can focus on improving skills like communication, providing feedback, and coaching. Each interaction with a team member is a chance to refine our interpersonal skills and cultivate meaningful relationships. LMX and the associated relationships can be leveraged by masterful leaders to drive organizational success.[1]

COLLABORATE: WORK WITH OTHERS TO MAKE A BIGGER IMPACT

Do you fully appreciate the abundance of human resources around you and know how to bring everyone's skills to bear? Interpersonally masterful people know how to encourage collaboration for the greater good. They're able to successfully communicate that the more ideas and talent one can bring to the table, the higher likelihood of true innovation and success.

Fostering an atmosphere of collaboration isn't easy. It's common for people to be protective of their ideas, to resist working on teams, and to operate in silos. How can you get everyone working together? Here are two action items you can start using right now:

1. **RECOGNIZE, REWARD, AND CELEBRATE COLLABORATIVE BEHAVIOR.** When we notice and reward collaborative efforts, it sends a strong message about what we value. Encouraging collaboration doesn't mean we have to enroll the office in a weekend team-building activity. Instead, build your team every day by encouraging people to talk to one another. Be known for saying things like "Hey, Janet, I hear you're working on some new product developments. Bill, over in marketing, expressed some cool ideas yesterday. How about the three of us get together and talk about it?" The rela-

tionships we cultivate today may be key to our success tomorrow. All of our institutions are relationship based: organizations, government, business, sports teams, marriages, and all require collaboration.

2. **MANAGE YOUR AGREEMENTS AND BE PRESENT.** I am continually advising my clients, "Don't agree to do something you know you don't have the time to do." When we do say yes, then it's important to show up and be present. People will come to see us not just as reliable but as interested. Being clear on our goals and committing to things that support our values are cornerstones of collaboration. Keeping the promises we do make and maintaining our commitments are part of treating people with respect. They won't forget it.

People who advance to the leading edge of performance know the importance of interpersonal mastery. They constantly work to expand and leverage their connections, communication, and collaboration. It's a choice to be conscious about the relationships we build. In the end, it's about creating a supportive environment for everyone to put their unique superpowers to the best possible use.

If you want to improve areas of your interpersonal mastery, here are some additional suggested actions you can start taking now to make a difference in how you establish and leverage your relationships to get more done and foster goodwill among those around you:

- **BUILD TRUST.** Maintain confidentiality and create an environment where it's safe to express opinions and ideas and to *fail.* People give you their best when they feel heard and respected.
- **BUILD AN INTERNAL SUPPORT SYSTEM.** Make it clear you and your colleagues are all on the same team. Provide support and nurturance to others, and encourage them to do the same for their colleagues.
- **PRESERVE YOUR BRIDGES.** Don't burn them. The world is small, and the relationships you cultivate today could be critical to your success tomorrow.
- **ENABLE SUCCESS.** Transformational leaders create opportunities for others to succeed and gain recognition. Provide others with space to grow, and honor them when they reach milestones. Learning to delegate not only takes pressure off of you; it gives others an opportunity to rise to the occasion and develop their own leadership skills.
- **LEAD WITH YOUR HEART.** Be authentic. Be vulnerable. Be truthful. True courage in leadership means acknowledging you don't have all the answers and do need the support and expertise of others. Give people kindness and courtesy, and they will give it back.

MASTERY IN ACTION:
George H. W. Bush and Stephen K. Hacker, Dynamic Duo

We can build relationships by taking some risks.

By nature, I'm an introvert. Despite being an inexperienced networker, I spent much of my midthirties flying all over the world working as a transformation consultant in different organizations and speaking as an expert at professional conferences.

I had a PhD in industrial-organizational psychology, and I would stand up and present information and facilitate discussions about metrics, planning, statistics, and leadership. I was good at that. But even though I was an expert, I still lacked confidence in social settings. When meeting new people or networking, I was out of my comfort zone.

When I was only a few years out of graduate school, one of my mentors saw leadership potential in me and wanted to help me unleash it. As a developmental opportunity, he nominated me to serve on the board of directors of a performance excellence association.

While I served on that board, we invited former President George H.W. Bush to speak at our annual conference. President Bush delivered a powerful motivational speech and encouraged all of us to go out and make a difference in our communities by connecting, communicating, and collaborating with others. Board members were invited to the reception that followed his keynote—a difficult event for a young introvert. I wanted to speak with him, but I was nervous.

I invited one of my colleagues, Stephen Hacker, who was attending the conference, to join me at the reception as my guest. We opened the door to the reception, looked in, and there was President Bush standing alone. People were milling around the periphery of the room, but no one had approached him.

Stephen knew immediately that something needed to be done. He grabbed my elbow and led me toward the middle of the room. I whispered, "You do the talking." When we reached President Bush, Stephen said, "President Bush, I'm Stephen Hacker, and this is Dr. Marta Wilson. She plans to present Senator Warner with some innovative ideas." Senator John Warner was a sponsor of the award, but I didn't actually know him yet. However, as a board member, I was prepared to put some new ideas in front of him.

I froze. Stephen had tossed out a proverbial ball to break the tension in the air. I could have easily caught it. Instead, I blushed. So, President Bush caught the ball and said, "So, you have some innovative challenges for John, have you? Great, he needs some new challenges!" Then he smiled. I breathed a sigh of relief.

A couple of people wandered over, and then a few

more people joined our little group. As they approached, President Bush said, "Everybody, Marta has some new ideas to suggest to John Warner. Isn't that great?" He included and involved me. After about the third time being introduced this way, I built up some courage and said with a smile, "I'm doing my best to make a difference." With the help of President Bush's interpersonally masterful style, my tension fell away.

The reception was a success, and when it ended, Stephen and I walked out together. I said, "Stephen, if you ever do that to me again—" Suddenly, I stopped and asked, "Do you have time to sit and talk with me? I want to be more effective."

Up to that point, I had been attached to being the expert. Stephen acknowledged my expertise, but he also suggested that perhaps I was withholding my unique superpowers and hiding my inner superhero. I walked away from that conversation and made a commitment to grow. I would no longer let my introversion be an excuse for not being, doing, or having something.

The more we work to educate ourselves about the people in our lives, the more we can walk into any situation, be at ease, and help others do the same. In the end, we can strive to connect, communicate, and collaborate with people. President Bush and Stephen Hacker are examples of such mastery. And sometimes, on my best days, now so am I.

BRINGING IT ALL TOGETHER

When we think about interpersonal mastery, it's about connecting, communicating, and collaborating with other people, and we can all do it in our own ways. Some people use humor. Some people use a smile. Some people are able to walk in and just light up a room. Everyone's different.

The more personally masterful we work to become by educating ourselves about the people and places in our lives, the more we can walk into any situation, be at ease, and help others do the same. In the end, we can choose to leverage our relationships by taking some risks to connect, communicate, and collaborate with others.

Questions for Reflection, Discovery, and Action

1. In what ways do you currently connect with others? What might be holding you back from making stronger connections? List three things.
2. What are three things you could try this week to work on making connections with more people in your workplace?
3. How do you communicate with others to achieve shared goals?
4. In what ways could you improve your communication skills at work? List three steps to start taking this week.
5. What are you currently doing to foster goodwill on your team, build rapport with individuals, and find common ground? Could you improve your skills in this area? Note three ways you could enhance your collaboration with your colleagues or clients this week.
6. Do you encourage people to collaborate? If so, list three tactics you currently use. Then list three things you will try this month to foster even greater collaboration in your workplace.

6

BOOST YOUR ORGANIZATIONAL MASTERY

In 2016, my company was awarded a multiyear, multimillion-dollar contract to provide management solutions across a large federal agency. The client organization has more than seven hundred thousand employees. Our mission on this contract was to launch an initiative to help members of the client workforce become more effective as total-systems thinkers, expand their potential to integrate elements of their work environment, and boost their organizational mastery. This effort would not only include TSI's LEAP program but also leverage one of our facilitation solutions known as VIEW, which stands for Visualize and Integrate Elements of the Workforce. VIEW facilitators help leaders make decisions using their own data-visualization systems that display results and activities for people, processes, and products.

As a small company, we were thrilled, honored, and excited when we were awarded this contract. Immediately, I sat down with my colleagues to discuss the contract kickoff. We realized that our team had been given an opportunity to make a difference in the lives of many people. Also, we knew it was a challenge that might change us and expand our wisdom as part of the experience. Not only were we embarking upon a transformation journey that potentially involved thousands of people, but there were thousands of processes and products in the mix. It was a bit overwhelming, but we were (and are) intentional about stretching together to embrace big new challenges.

When TSI works with an organization, we have a few senior leaders within that organization who are our main points of contact. They are our clients and our advocates throughout the duration of the engagement. On this contract, our most senior point of contact was an executive we'll call Kate (in order to protect her privacy). We met Kate through one of our long-term clients, which we began supporting in 2006. This client believed enough in the success we had accomplished with their one hundred employees to introduce us to Kate in order to help thousands of people across several commands within this large organization's total enterprise.

At contract launch, Kate asked us to start by meeting with her top one hundred leaders. So, we met with the most senior leaders within every command to describe what we were offering and, most importantly, to ask them what they needed. As my team and I trekked through the sleet and snow of that fall and winter to visit all of these leaders, we experienced an adventure ranging from having the red carpet rolled out for us at some locations to walking half a mile in a hailstorm on one memorable occasion. Some leaders welcomed us and the solutions we were offering. Some admitted they were so focused on basic needs such as facilities that they couldn't see leveraging our help at that time.

As always, we were looking for early adopters and went where the energy led us in order to get the contract off to a great start. One early adopter said to us, "This is like a lick of a free ice cream cone. We'll taste it, and if we like it, we'll buy a gallon in the future." Soon, we began working closely with them to create meetings, workshops, products, and plans that they found valuable—with eventual successes they could share with their peers. This created a lot of peer pressure for other leaders to help them do the same thing. All the while, we kept Kate informed of every move we made throughout her total system.

One important thing our team did on this contract was to get these one hundred leaders together to talk to one another, sometimes all at once and sometimes in subgroups of ten to twelve people. We brought them together in our client's data visualization rooms where they could see multiple briefs, quarterly reports, and other various charts all at once. With our VIEW facilitation framework, we made sure these leaders were always surrounded by data and information about what was and wasn't working within their total system. This interactive process was valuable for our clients.

At one point, one of these working groups decided that members of their enterprise-wide career field needed a certain type of training, and they announced this at one of Kate's larger hundred-leader meetings. It turned out that about seven other working groups needed the same training and had been looking at other vendors. In that meeting, with Kate's encouragement and display of organizational mastery, all these working groups decided to only buy this training once, which resulted in increased efficiencies in the procurement process, saving time and energy. This decision translated into a significant cost savings, and they only had to go through the procurement process one time instead of seven times. Bravo, Kate!

During the meetings that our team facilitated for Kate and her leaders, it became clear there were opportunities to better manage the people in Kate's workforce in a very systematic way. For example, employees were on a number of different pay systems, they were spread all across the country, and they weren't getting enough career-development guidance. As more opportunities came to light, Kate acted as an integrator of the many moving parts in her organization. She encouraged one command that was the best at developing and delivering timely training tailored to their workforce to tweak it so that it could be scalable and applied to other commands. Then, she asked the leaders of this command to share the training with other commands. As a result, the initial command became a hero by making excellent training available to five times as many people as before—with no extra development or procurement costs. Again, bravo, Kate!

Recently, my team and I were discussing what we've observed about Kate as a leader in working with her. Our main takeaway is that Kate is a total-systems thinker. She understands that getting outstanding products to end users not only requires solid processes; it also requires supporting the people inside those processes. Kate is an example of organizational mastery in motion, and we are honored to support her as a leader.

ORGANIZATIONAL MASTERY: TOTAL-SYSTEMS THINKERS

Like Kate, the most effective people see the big picture. They grasp how actions by one person can affect many others. Those who have such a grasp and fully utilize what such a vision can bring to their organizations demonstrate organizational mastery. They are the people who advance to the leading edge of performance. They are driven to be total-systems thinkers, and have carefully studied strategies for integrating people, products, and processes. Systems thinkers have knowledge of how all the moving parts of their organization work together as part of the whole.

THE MOST EFFECTIVE PEOPLE SEE THE BIG PICTURE.

Individuals with organizational mastery exhibit an understanding of how their enterprises work at the proverbial thirty-thousand-foot level, recognizing how different factors influence one another yet demonstrating the ability to communicate these enterprise-wide realizations to people with clarity. Balancing vision and communication of that vision is a rare quality but one that can be learned if you dedicate yourself to doing so. Once you do, the people within your sphere of influence will start to see the big picture and how they, as individuals, contribute to the vision.

Winning leaders enable their workforces to achieve big, bold goals. This requires a mindful and conscious shift in perspective and action, one that relies upon a powerful vision that includes engaging people at all levels. Without such vision, performance-improvement efforts will go nowhere. Where do effective leaders begin when it comes to helping people to visualize the kinds of goals that can transform an organization and maximize its ability to compete? Three ways they do this include (1) bringing people together—not just employees, but customers, suppliers, and others—to the organizational mission; (2) sharing the big picture, creating certainty that everyone understands the context of system-wide goals; and (3) clarifying the score for all involved, making certain measures are in place, so everyone knows how close they are to hitting their targets and helping everybody understand the total system.

When we discuss organizational mastery, the key is integration among people, processes, and products.

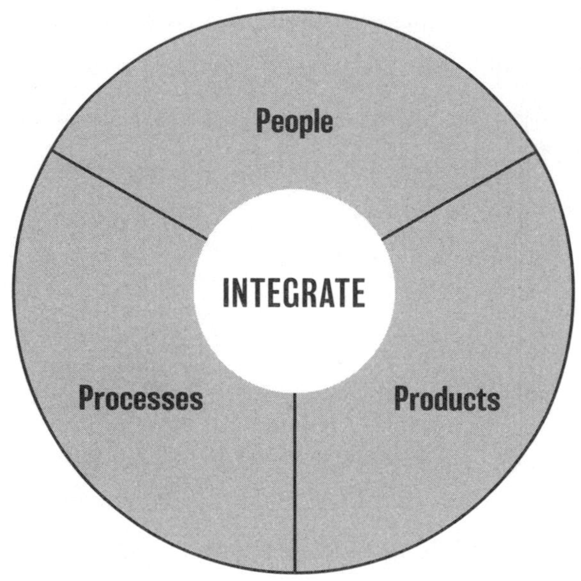

Kate is an outstanding example of someone who is an integrator—and why it can matter so greatly. Challenges like those Kate faced become ever more complicated in modern business models where employees are spread at a distance, and whole systems are connected by rapidly changing technologies. It's unlikely you have thousands of employees supporting end users across the globe, yet your organizational challenges are every bit as real and pressing. As you havc probably noticed, organizations continue to become more networked. With sophisticated networks, more virtual work environments, greater numbers of remote employees, and other technological innovations, our dependence on these integrated systems continues to grow and stretches the connecting bonds among our people. We become increasingly reliant on the employees within our organizations who possess technological expertise, creative-minded communication skills, and systems vision. But this reliance also creates opportunity and reemphasizes the impact individuals can have on the larger enterprise.

The first step to unleashing the potential of individuals to improve your total organization is to get some concept of your enterprise as a working system, a total system. In one way or other, various models all tease out distinct parts of the whole system, providing a starting point for how change in one area can affect people and processes throughout the organization.

Understanding your suppliers, inputs, people, processes, products, outputs, clients, and outcomes is another important step in improving your organization. When you see how one person can have organization-wide impact and how one task can have enterprise-wide effect, you can improve functionality across the board. Whenever we face a large-scale problem, we can begin by looking for changes that will solve many problems, and seize many opportunities, throughout the organization.

Transformational leaders convey a unifying vision. This vision represents shared values and connects individuals to the work they do. A vision often includes overtones that convey the deeper meaning or greater good served by the commodity produced or service provided. This vision acts as a unifying call to action. It connects people to tasks, tasks to processes, processes to products, and products to customers—creating a captivating narrative. What masterful leaders must do is involve everyone in the organizational family in a shared vision and inspire consensus that today's sacrifices are worth tomorrow's payoff.

When faced with a dauntingly complex system, we can create greater levels of possibility and performance if we master integrating people, processes, and products.

PEOPLE: PULSATING HEART OF AN INTEGRATED ORGANIZATION

One person taking one action can have organization-wide value in businesses, churches, charities, schools—organizations of every kind—and even at home. That's why it's important to remember the special value of the human element in total systems. The human level is where continuous improvement occurs in organizations. Successful and influential leaders draw on each person's fluency in his or her area of the total system in order to improve the whole. The best models

SUCCESSFUL AND INFLUENTIAL LEADERS DRAW ON EACH PERSON'S FLUENCY IN HIS OR HER AREA OF THE TOTAL SYSTEM IN ORDER TO IMPROVE THE WHOLE.

for organizing systems reflect how the total organization can improve when one person or group gets smarter, reaches a benchmark, or employs a bright innovation.

Because people are so essential to understanding how total systems work, it's important to consider all the stakeholders—all the *people*—involved in different aspects of the system. Obviously, we have to talk about the people directly within the organization—the employees that make its heart beat—but we cannot talk about processes without talking about some other people, namely suppliers, and we cannot talk about products unless we talk about end users—our customers. These are but two groups of people who must be directly involved when considering the human face of the three organizational mastery components.

In this chapter on organizational mastery, I offer some tips to help you integrate the people, processes, and products of your environment. These are drawn from my book *Everybody's Business*, where you can find a number of other practical applications. When considering the people component of total-systems thinking, consider these two actions:

1. **LIST AND CONSIDER LONG-TERM AND SHORT-TERM OUTCOMES OF YOUR DECISIONS.** Some things feel good now but bad later. Leaders take a *long-term view*. Certainly, from time to time they may set aside

a grander view to complete a project on time and on budget. Largely, however, leaders balance schedule and quality with people's needs. They understand how retention and engagement serve the organization as well as its employees over time.

2. **DRAW ON PEOPLE'S STRENGTHS TO BENEFIT THE WHOLE ORGANIZATION.** Part of considering people's needs also has the benefit of being able to seek their feedback. We can see the long view better with multiple viewpoints, and the cultivated relationships of interpersonal mastery can help us accomplish organizational mastery by having others help us see the broader needs of the organization. It can also help us assess its greatest strengths and growth opportunities.

MASTERY IN ACTION:

John Mackey—Seeing the Big Picture and Making a Difference

I divide my time between my apartment in the city and house in the country. One of my favorite perks of the urban half of my life is living within walking distance of a Whole Foods Market. I'm a regular customer and appreciate having a large selection of healthy foods just steps away. As someone who founded my own company, I'm always curious to learn the stories of other inspiring company founders who have led their organizations to extraordinary levels of success. The story of John Mackey, the cofounder and CEO of Whole Foods, is one of these. He borrowed $45,000 to open his first health food store in 1978 and has since revolutionized the organic-food industry with more than 450 Whole Foods locations. Under Mackey's leadership, Whole Foods was acquired in 2017 by Amazon for $13.7 billion. He understood customer wants before most realized such customers even existed. Mackey is organizational mastery in motion, and his mastery has led to record-breaking results for Whole Foods.

Much of Mackey's success has been due to his strong understanding and advocacy for total-systems thinking. He's spent his career focusing on what his customers want, but also on the way the Whole Foods footprint impacts the larger system of food production and distribution. He doesn't just pay attention to food once it hits the store shelves, or even just one step prior, to ensure it meets organic standards. Rather, Mackey steps all the way back and monitors factors among their suppliers, such as energy conservation, waste reduction, soil health, and farmworker welfare. In fact, in 2014 he rolled out a new rating system called Responsibly Grown to measure these elements. Talk about seeing the "whole" picture. Mackey was thinking about "farm to table" long before it gained popular appeal among restaurateurs with far-reaching results. Now, that is organizational mastery in action!

Mackey is a vocal advocate for what he calls "conscious

capitalism," which is a way of doing business that attempts to create value for all stakeholders—employees, customers, suppliers, investors, the community, and the environment. It's an approach to business that fulfills the deepest purpose of the organization while creating value for the entire interdependent system. Mackey, alongside other thinkers and corporate leaders, was a central figure in the development of principles that form conscious capitalism and at implementing those principles into modern business. After giving talks and interviews and writing white papers that began to define the concepts, Mackey, together with coauthor Raj Sisodia, wrote the book *Conscious*.

The website of Conscious Capitalism Inc., an organization with close ties to Mackey and dedicated to further developing the principles he advocated in his book and through his work, offers a great working definition for conscious capitalism in their credo:

> "Conscious Capitalism" is a way of thinking about capitalism and business that better reflects where we are in the human journey, the state of our world today, and the innate potential of business to make a positive impact on the world. Conscious businesses are galvanized by higher purposes that serve, align and integrate the interests of all their major stakeholders. Their

> higher state of consciousness makes visible to them the interdependencies that exist across all stakeholders, allowing them to discover and harvest synergies from situations that otherwise seem replete with trade-offs.[1]

Mackey goes on to suggest that the leaders of such conscious-minded organizations are driven by service to the company's purpose, to all the people the business touches, and to the planet. As a result, in his eyes, "conscious businesses have trusting, authentic, innovative, and caring cultures that make working there a source of both personal growth and professional fulfillment."[2]

I admire Mackey's wide-scale and far-reaching vision of what organizations can do when they, as expressed in Conscious Capitalism Inc.'s credo, "endeavor to create financial, intellectual, social, cultural, emotional, spiritual, physical, and ecological wealth for all their stakeholders." And I am moved to see more leaders taking John Mackey's approach. More and more companies include the health of the planet, the sustainability of their business, and the well-being of their stakeholders as part of their measurement for organizational success. Increasingly, we are seeing more evidence that such businesses significantly outperform traditional businesses in their bottom line, all while creating rich, vibrant, and, yes, "conscious" enterprises.

PROCESSES: CIRCULATORY SYSTEMS OF AN ORGANIZATION

By their very nature, processes, particularly those in large, multifaceted enterprises, can become complicated. We need to find clear approaches to managing them. Using a model to describe complexity can be a great asset for such organizations.

Over time, in many industries, the SIPOC model (an acronym for suppliers, inputs, processes, outputs, customers) has successfully guided assessment activities in full-throttle organizations. SIPOC is not alone as a model for whole-systems-oriented organizations, and other models are helpful in different ways. But all good models reflect research taking place in new working environments, and nearly all total-systems models emphasize a central role for people. SIPOC, for example, is largely about human beings. The central truth is that we cannot talk meaningfully about processes unless we recognize that people are the key components within them. SIPOC, like other tools, is an attempt to bring order into what are inherently complex systems, and, thereby, systems that can too easily fall into chaos or suffer misdirected action—or inaction.

For example, picture the difficulty of trying to get an organization the size, importance, and complexity of the US Navy to find a common mission when diverse enterprise stakeholders have different and perhaps conflicting demands that drive priorities. Imagine the polarity faced daily among people within the warfighting system and the acquisition system when naval air operations hardware aboard an aircraft carrier stationed across the globe requires significant engineering changes that must work their way through the red tape of a DC-based accounting division. One part of the transaction requires agile, adaptable, rapid technology development and is dependent on another division that must continuously battle through methodical, rigid, politicized government regulations and processes. For my team at TSI, not only is it important to find models that help both groups communicate and achieve their needs, it's also important to offer solutions that help all stakeholders see how they all serve the larger institutional purpose. SIPOC and other tools can help people system-wide recognize that the entire enterprise is made up of people with wildly divergent personalities. Indeed, while we need models like SIPOC and others to manage such complex systems, they require capable, mission-focused people to make them work.

The performance of suppliers has profound impact on enterprise success and a direct one in managing processes. Suppliers' first-hand experience of an organization's work effectiveness can provide feedback that moves from the point of contact all the way to affecting choices in product design or directions in service expertise. Suppliers are particularly central as strategic partners—and sources of market information.

For example, in the shipbuilding industry, suppliers can help to inform Navy leaders on newly emerging technologies and cost-saving possibilities that help the Navy's budgeting process. The suppliers inform purchasers about their products and services and share new findings in research and development that are about to come to market. Key partners can bring their expertise to bear and create solutions to support success, if we take the time to explain to them our business needs and goals.

Two suggestions to boost process excellence include the following:

1. **PLAN STRATEGICALLY.** Use planning tools to set goals, do important work, and have meaningful success. The well-crafted strategic plan can become a valuable playbook, although its development can take some time. The goal is clarity, and the process can be energizing. What you have, in the end, is a shared understanding that becomes a familiar reference point.

2. **SPEND TIME ON WHAT-IF SCENARIOS.** The more time we spend testing processes on the front end, the less rework we have to do on the back end, and the better the outcome will be.

THROUGH THE LENS OF SCIENCE:
Dr. Deming's Profound Knowledge

W. Edwards Deming was an engineer, author, lecturer, and thought leader who pioneered our modern understanding of systems thinking. In his book *Out of Crisis* (1982), Deming put forth the Theory of Profound Knowledge, which is comprised of four main components: appreciation of a system, theory of knowledge, psychology of change, and knowledge about variation.

1. Appreciation of a system depends on a leader's ability to understand the interconnectedness and interdependence of the different people, products, and processes of an organization.
2. Theory of knowledge refers to the idea that improvement of a system can only come from iterations of performance and reflection.
3. The psychology of change states that a system self-organizes around its identity. It is the responsibility of leaders to create a vision and help to guide people around this vision to facilitate organizational identity and performance.
4. Knowledge of variation is the understanding that no two things are identical: not people, not products, not processes. Understanding these differences and predicting behavior are key to a leader's ability to remove problems or barriers in the system.

Dr. Deming posited that people were an asset to be leveraged, not an expense to be managed. Great leaders understand this and put effort into using an individual's unique talents within processes to facilitate an effective system. These leaders understand how to leverage intrinsic motivation and remove obstacles inhibiting success. Transformational leaders heed the wisdom of Deming; they, at their core, are enablers of success in others.

PRODUCTS: ENERGY OUTPUT THROUGH GOODS AND SERVICES

Customers are a great source for ideas to improve products and services. But many organizations don't have a sufficient dialogue in place to discover ideas from customers' unique vantage points. In the DoD, warfighters are constantly being surveyed, interviewed, and canvassed to discover what they are experiencing as the end users of the technology, weapon systems, and general supplies—whether those supplies are missiles, aviator sunglasses, phone systems for calling home, or the onions for tonight's recipe in the mess hall. The only way to know how to make improvements is to gather data and give feedback to suppliers and other parts of the total system. This makes the lives of the frontline military personnel better, and in the end, can save lives.

The kind of total-systems thinking required to be effective has to be face-to-face and hands-on when possible and must be conducted with sincerity and purpose. An example of this occurred when the TSI team provided engineering management support to a customer in charge of installing an in-vehicle computer network in a mine-resistant armored truck. After installing a network in a working truck, our team conducted a day-long user evaluation with eight members of the US Marine Corps. The Marines put the truck through its paces using the new network interface and then talked about what worked well and what should be improved. Our team documented what they heard and had the Marines review their notes. Reflecting on the process, our project team leader said, "The Marines' feedback made this project more than installing an in-vehicle network; we were developing integrated controls, computing, and displays for warfighters to more efficiently manage their next generation of in-vehicle systems."

Here are two product-oriented actions to consider when applying total-systems thinking:

1. **CONNECT PEOPLE WITH PRODUCTS AND OUTCOMES.** Aligning individual and organizational results will boost both. We must rely on strong and open discussion with everyone who has a role in our enterprise if we are to succeed in taking a pulse on the current state of our total system.
2. **MEASURE, AND MEASURE AGAIN.** One of my favorite sayings is "Inspect what you expect." For example, it's critical to continuously talk with our customers and make certain we are meeting their needs and expectations. We all need a steady stream of meaningful data and a clear bar to raise or change as we adapt.

In the example of our team's experience working in the defense industry, we saw direct input from the suppliers installing the equipment, the end users of the network, and through TSI as the consultant, a direct line of report back to the procurement specialists purchasing the equipment. This is total-systems thinking in action.

The same need for feedback applies to employees and contractors in all organizations. Add to these the other stakeholders who interact with the organization in any way, from investors and media to the community service groups with whom staff may volunteer, and we have a huge resource pool of feedback to draw upon. Every stakeholder has something to say worth hearing. If we can listen to enough of them and have mechanisms in place for analyzing what we hear and forming action plans from it, their insights offer a comprehensive image of the total system at work. Here is where the quality of leadership is tested, even reworked. To begin, it's important to listen with an open mind to reviews both good and bad. We incorporate surveys, focus groups, one-on-one interviews, and user conferences as tools within our own company and our client organizations to gather feedback and to connect, communicate, and collaborate with suppliers, customers, employees, and others. Sometimes it's as simple as picking up the phone.

EVERY STAKEHOLDER HAS SOMETHING TO SAY WORTH HEARING.

Leaders who are effective at gathering stakeholder

perceptions also inspire others to think beyond their current domain of responsibility and gain a clearer knowledge of the greater system in which they work. This way, leaders inspire a total-systems mind-set in others. The effects of organizational mastery can become exponential as a result. As a first step, I suggest getting a grip on your total system and beginning to understand the unique human factor that can create solutions for your organization's growth and change.

Developing organizational mastery comes down to being committed to having clarity, discovering insight, and showing respect for all of the elements within our environment. It requires a passion for understanding all of the moving parts and how they work (or don't work) together. We can consciously look for ways to integrate the elements of our organization, including people, processes, and products, and can actively understand, support, and leverage them. As part of this, it's important to understand the vision of organizations we support and recognize where we can be catalysts of transformation. Properly harnessed, the superpowers of becoming a total-systems thinker can have enormous and lasting impacts and help our organizations soar.

Developing organizational mastery can be challenging, because it requires understanding disparate pieces of an enterprise and how each of those pieces ultimately plays a role in customer satisfaction. You can, however, grow your organizational mastery. Here are some additional suggested actions:

- **EMPOWER PEOPLE.** When your team members have more authority, knowledge, and support, they will do more for the organization. Give them the power to act.
- **STRIVE FOR CONTINUOUS IMPROVEMENT.** Don't settle. Always look for ways to make things better. Monitor the integration of suppliers, inputs, processes, outputs, and customers to find new opportunities for improvement. Realize that something that worked a year ago may not be the best for today … or tomorrow.
- **BE FLEXIBLE.** Respect the policies and processes that are in place, but also exercise your skill at finding better and more efficient ways to meet goals while still achieving compliance.
- **APPRECIATE PERSPECTIVE.** Honor diverse viewpoints within your organization, and use them to find new and better ways of meeting goals. Dissent is not the enemy. Foster dialogue and problem-solving.

DISSENT IS NOT THE ENEMY. FOSTER DIALOGUE AND PROBLEM-SOLVING.

- **GET BUY-IN.** This is especially critical when making department- or organization-wide changes in processes and the information technology that supports them. Bring all the stakeholders to the table, not just part of the team. Make sure everyone understands what the goals are and the effort required to achieve them.

- **BE CONSISTENT.** Document roles, processes, and product specifications to help with training and to provide a starting point for continuous improvement. Documentation also clarifies expectations and helps team members understand what success looks like within the roles they occupy.
- **DRIVE COMMITMENT TO PRODUCT EXCELLENCE.** Make sure everyone in the organization understands how your products and/or services create value for your customers, and make sure everyone is committed to product excellence and the reputation building that follows it.

MASTERY IN ACTION:
Steve Forbes and Janelle Millard, Two Total-Systems Thinkers

Successful individuals create linkages among people, processes, and products.

A few years ago I attended an event where executives were auctioned to raise money for charity. Lunch with Steve Forbes, chairman of Forbes Media, was up for auction. Janelle Millard, the director of strategic initiatives at my company, advised me to bid on Steve. Her intent was to expand our business, grow our publishing arm, and strengthen our brand. So, I bid, and guess what? I WON.

I met Steve for lunch in New York. When we were seated, to my surprise, I noticed my three books on the chair beside him. He told me that he had scanned my books, visited my Twitter page, and read my blog. Steve asked some questions about my company, and I realized he already knew a lot about our clients, our solutions, and how we generate revenue. He understood my business.

He offered many helpful suggestions, such as writing a book that sums up my previous books. He said that a *Fortune* 100 CEO or federal executive could read it quickly, potentially piquing their interest in my leadership development program. Steve also suggested that I develop an app that could help people become more effective leaders.

Steve generously shared insight and advice. He helped me think through developing new products and new processes. He encouraged me to think about all of my company's inputs, throughputs, and outputs from a different angle.

Steve helped me imagine possibilities for my company to expand our client base, grow our publishing arm, and strengthen our brand recognition. During our discussion, I even started to envision going global, and it felt possible. By the time we had finished lunch, my mind was racing!

I flew home that afternoon, and the next morning I met with Janelle. I briefed her on all of Steve's suggestions. Janelle's response was, "We can do it, Marta. I'm ready if you are!" Janelle helped me analyze all of Steve's guidance, and she kept an open mind as if each and every suggestion was a possibility. Together, we prepared to implement some new ideas.

We hosted a series of executive forums bringing together CEOs from a wide variety of industries. These roundtables were a big success and led to many introductions into new client organizations.

Two years after lunch with Steve, the LEAP app was ready to launch, and the draft manuscript of my book *LEAP* was complete. Janelle and I reached out to Steve and invited him to lunch, where we gave him an update, telling him we had implemented all of his ideas. He was surprised and delighted.

Steve can take any business and analyze its individual parts. He leveraged a lifetime of experience and distilled it into nuggets that I could use. He could have just shown up and made small talk. Instead, he invested his time and shared his wisdom. From it, I've seen possibilities within my business I would not have realized.

Janelle took the initiative to influence me to bid on the lunch with Steve. That was powerful. Where we find leadership in our lives is not always in the places that we're looking. Janelle led me. She motivated me. I followed her, and then with Steve's suggestions, she led me to make investments to do bigger things and set bolder goals. Today, I look to Janelle for vision and innovation. In this story both Steve and Janelle exhibited organizational mastery and helped me make a bigger difference in my sphere of influence.

With Janelle's encouragement and Steve's wisdom, I became more organizationally masterful. In the end, the combined energy and thoughtfulness of three generations created some amazing results. Thank you, Janelle and Steve.

BRINGING IT ALL TOGETHER

Sometimes we don't see the leader sitting right beside us or allow ourselves to support someone else's leadership. There's magic when we do.

Organizational mastery is understanding our system and how we fit into the big picture. It's constantly looking for ways to improve people, processes, and products. Organizational mastery is looking for ways to make a bigger difference in our spheres of influence.

Questions for Reflection, Discovery, and Action

1. What are some new or novel ways I could experiment with in order to integrate the various elements of my work environment, including people, processes, and products?
2. In what ways do I demonstrate my understanding of and support for the roles people play throughout my organization? What else could I do that I haven't done before?
3. How do I gather ideas from my customers, coworkers, and stakeholders? What could I do differently to be more effective in seeking information from others?
4. How am I connected to the processes within my workplace? How do I add value to those processes?
5. Where do I excel in creating stellar products? If I tapped into my superpowers, how could I improve the outputs I'm responsible for producing?
6. What is my understanding of the vision for my organization? How would I summarize it in one sentence?
7. What are some concrete ways that I demonstrate I am a total-systems thinker?

7

MAGNIFY YOUR MOTIVATIONAL MASTERY

In the previous chapter I described some aspects of TSI's work on a contract providing transformational solutions across a large enterprise. In addition to helping boost organizational mastery with the help of our VIEW facilitation approach, we were also invited to pilot the workforce-development program LEAP that is the focus of this book.

Our client Kate wanted to see if LEAP could help members of her workforce become more personally, interpersonally, organizationally, and motivationally masterful. She wanted to invest in energizing her workforce. That's what our program is designed to do—help individuals make choices to change their lives, discover their unique superpowers, and unleash those inner superheroes. Specifically, with respect to motivational mastery, as we started to deliver keynotes, workshops, and summits for Kate's organization, we saw that it helped people overcome their fear of speaking up by providing just enough structure and support so that they felt safe in opening the blinds a bit on their challenges without fear that their peers and colleagues were going to judge them.

The LEAP program creates a psychologically safe environment that helps people at all levels of the organization engage, elevate, and energize one another, regardless of whether they are new to their field or they've seen it all throughout a long career. A benefit that my team brings to our client organizations when implementing a LEAP program is the fact that we are outsiders to their system. Therefore, we bring an objective perspective that allows leaders at all levels to open up not only with us but also in larger and larger groups of their peers. As this phenomenon evolves, people's ability to inspire one another expands, and they become more motivationally masterful.

When people become more motivationally masterful, one way we see them engage, elevate, and energize others more effectively is through showing vulnerability. Based on our observations, this includes less posturing and less putting a constant spin on the situation that everything is "green." As people become more motivationally masterful, their willingness to say things are not perfect but instead are "yellow" moving to "red" becomes more prevalent. They stop saying, "Leave me alone. I can handle this." They begin saying, "Our results aren't all that great. We could use some help." For example, we saw leaders begin to admit that they needed to fix the length of time required by their hiring cycle. If they failed to improve the process, they realized they would not land the talent they needed for the future. Once the problem was out in the open, solutions began to emerge through focused conversations and were quickly implemented. We love to see these kinds of results.

With motivationally masterful leaders in place, we see teams asking more probing but nonjudgmental questions. For instance, "Can you tell me more about that? Are others experiencing the same thing? What have you tried?" We also see a fair amount of humor. Once the environment changes, I can't tell you how many times we've heard leaders say things like, "Well, that sounds dumb! Why do we do that?" Everybody laughs, and then the group decides to do things differently. We also see a lot more impatience about the pace of implementing action on decisions, with leaders becoming less likely to accept a long time line for anything. This is a useful attitude, especially across defense agencies, when you think about the many threats that our country faces with respect to national security.

Another motivational behavior we've observed is that Kate's boss (we'll call him Clark) encourages all of his senior leaders to take on something big in their domains. Typically, the nature of the organization is such that new ideas that can impact readiness or capability are implemented only if they have at least a 50 percent chance of success. He asks each of them to generate one idea per year that has a 50 percent risk of failure. Clark encourages smart risk-taking for the sake of speed. People find this inspiring, and Kate encourages this behavior in her top leaders. For example, she recently tasked a team to reduce hiring-cycle time to forty-five days, a policy that has a low probably of success given federal government constraints. But if it does succeed, it will have a huge impact. Kate then engaged a senior leader of one of her large multibillion-dollar divisions to take the helm on this challenge. When other leaders see this, it inspires them to take on bigger, bolder risks within their own domains of responsibility.

MOTIVATIONAL MASTERY: ENGAGE, ELEVATE, ENERGIZE

The role that our team and the LEAP program play in enabling people to take bigger, bolder goals begins with the assessments, coaching, mentoring, and training we provide to senior leaders. These types of interventions help leaders find their courage to behave differently, and there is a trickle-down effect as we see their people also adopting bolder goals. In addition, the leadership rules (see chapter 8) that we introduce create the conditions for our clients to engage, elevate, and energize one another in ways that many were not exhibiting before. I am amazed at the effective leadership we have witnessed being displayed by so many of our valued clients over the past few years, and it's rewarding to see the difference our team has made in helping them put motivational mastery in motion.

As Kate's and Clark's examples illustrate, people who advance to the leading edge of performance have motivational mastery. They engage, elevate, and energize others. They are driven to think, decide, and act in ways that lift and inspire people, and they create an environment where people are motivated to do their best work and perform with excellence. Effective leaders motivate their colleagues by supporting sustainable achievement of individual and organizational goals. By motivating everyone in this way, leaders are better able to mentor and accelerate people's professional development and alignment with the organization.

Great leaders are inspirational, because they keep the mission of the entire enterprise in their sights and recognize how they can motivate others to do the same by engaging, elevating, and energizing them. Let's look at each of these three key elements in more depth. For each component, I'll also offer some advice I've found through working alongside inspirational colleagues and partners. These nuggets of acquired wisdom can be found, along with many more, in my book *Energized Enterprise*.

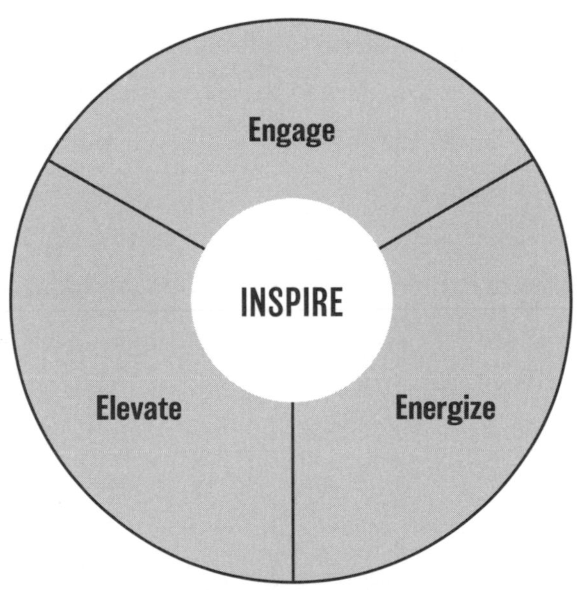

ENGAGE: REACH OUT FOR SUCCESS

Influential leaders include and involve everyone in the story that's unfolding within their organizations. I often recall an example from one of my clients, Dave, who oversaw national warehouses that supplied products to grocery stores. When a large competitor threatened to move into their market, Dave had to figure out a way to increase efficiency by 30 percent to prevent losing market share to the new competition. This client was masterful about communicating a larger story, encouraging everyone in all of the warehouses to band together to save the company's market share and drive out the competition. He prefaced every communication, from emails to meetings to water cooler conversations, with the story of the company's heritage and succeeded in tying that history to the big picture. Soon all the employees knew the story and then participated in sharing it with others. Dave had successfully created a collective identity. He took this communication a step further and painted a metaphorical picture of a burning platform. In other words, he made sure everyone knew that the organization had to change, or the platform around it would

INFLUENTIAL LEADERS INCLUDE AND INVOLVE EVERYONE IN THE STORY THAT'S UNFOLDING WITHIN THEIR ORGANIZATIONS.

burn, and then they would have no choice but to change. Their mission was to accept the need for transformation while preserving the company's legacy. Our client recognized that sometimes you have no choice but to change if you are to survive. Whether something positive is pulling us or something negative is pushing us, we have to make the bigger picture everybody's motivation, and we must be selective in our efforts to achieve it.

Two suggestions for engaging others include the following:

1. **UNDERSTAND PEOPLE.** People are your greatest asset; treat them that way. People are the most important factor in every enterprise, no matter how large or how small. Notice people who offer a contribution and thank them. Embrace your own humanity as well, and let your emotions shine. Smile, laugh, and have fun with your team. Ask people what they're thinking.
2. **ACTIVELY CARE ABOUT PEOPLE.** Effective leaders show an interest in people. This interest doesn't have to be limited to work goals. If a person wants to learn about something that's not under his or her job description, consider creating some flexibility to figure out a way to integrate those personal interests with the job in a way that benefits the organization. Another way to really show you care is to absorb the stress from above. Even though it's important

to be transparent and authentic, our team does not always need to feel all of the pressures that we feel from every stakeholder. They can be more effective when we do not pass down too many emotional burdens. Despite difficult pressures, effective leaders remain focused, clear, and calm, which builds the confidence of everyone around them.

THROUGH THE LENS OF SCIENCE:
Learning by Observation

In the eleventh edition of their book *Psychology*, David G. Myers and C. Nathan DeWall help us understand the scientific underpinning behind why motivationally masterful people can become so profound in all of our lives. Basically, we can observe and learn. They write:

> In the field of psychology, observational learning is when humans learn without direct experience by watching and imitating others. We learn our native languages and various other specific behaviors by observing and imitating others, a process called modeling. Pioneering researcher of observational learning, Dr. Albert Bandura, conducted groundbreaking experiments in the 1960s that demonstrated the phenomenon of learning by modeling. Bandura discovered that by watching a model, we experience vicarious reinforcement or vicarious punishment, and we learn to anticipate a behavior's consequences in situations like those we are observing. We are especially likely to learn from people we perceive as similar to ourselves, as successful, or as admirable. Even our fears may extinguish as we observe another safely navigating the feared situation. Lord Chesterfield (1694–1773) had the idea: "We are, in truth, more than half what we are by imitation."[1]

ELEVATE: PUSH THE "UP" BUTTON TO HELP OTHERS EXCEL

As we saw with Dave's example, successful leaders retain reminders of the institutional mission in their communications. They make sure that everyone in their total system is reminded that what they do contributes to the organization's mission. My team once worked with a group that handled billing and processing. The leaders did a great job of identifying the mission of each department and the performance measures that matched those missions. They tracked them over time, then shared this information, educating the recipients so that everyone knew how to drive performance in a proactive, nonthreatening way. It raised the level of energy in the workforce. All the employees knew how those measures reflected performance to mission and how what they did each day drove those measures up or down. They started doing more with less, and productivity went through the roof.

In the past, the employees sometimes spent all day doing the wrong things. My team analyzed historical data to show that it didn't pay to go after the largest past-due bills first. The large past-due bills were often six months or more overdue, requiring a lot of time to find the account holders—if they could be found at all—and resulting in a small return on average.

After our consultation, they started doing the right things, and they could see an impact on the organization. We used a measure of expected value to show that an employee should go after the most recent past-due bills first. The account holders for more recent bills were easier to find, more likely to pay their overdue balances, and less likely to let the bills grow to an unmanageable amount. The result, shared daily with employees, was more revenue recovered per billing employee—good for team morale, performance, and the bottom line. Employees could see an impact on the organization. They understood the significance of their work and received regular feedback on it.

EFFECTIVE LEADERS HELP PEOPLE FIGURE OUT WHAT'S IMPORTANT, AND THEY MEASURE, REWARD, AND RECOGNIZE THOSE BEHAVIORS THAT SUPPORT IT.

This client's transformation demonstrates that everyone is a piece of the bigger picture. That means everyone should be doing something that they know is important. Effective leaders help people figure out what's important, and they measure, reward, and recognize those behaviors that support it.

Here are two ways to elevate others:

1. **DON'T PUNISH FAILURE.** Failure often reflects that new ideas were tried. Failure can be a badge of courage, because someone dared to take a risk. Failure supports excellence by allowing us to make corrections and stay on target. Let some time pass after failure occurs, and then ask people to reflect. Have them ask, "What can I do differently next time?" And in that spirit, have them regularly ask themselves, "What is the most important thing I did today?" The answers can help clarify a variety of values and motivations.

2. **REMEMBER, IT'S NOT JUST ABOUT THE MONEY.** Don't give up on motivation because you can't offer more money; money is not the only motivator. Other motivators include respect, appreciation, belonging, and accomplishing a mission. Study after study, particularly among millennials, shows that people put much greater value on being in environments where they can learn, move up, and be respected than they do on salary alone.

ENERGIZE: CULTIVATING COLLECTIVE POTENTIAL

Effective leaders plant and cultivate seeds of energy. Such leaders display energy themselves, and openly, authentically, demonstrate genuine interest in the people they lead. People become a reflection of the attitudes, traits, and behaviors that leaders display. In an energized enterprise led by an effective leader, we see possibility thinkers who say, "Sure, we can do that!" or "How can we do that?" Their attitudes are, "We've got one another's backs." People offer help when they know you need it or even if they are not sure you need it. They work in an atmosphere of optimism, and they have a high level of self-confidence. They're awake, alive, alert, and open to one another's needs and the requirements of the larger organization. They're always wondering what's next. They're never satisfied or content with the status quo. They're thinking about how to move on to better or different things. They laugh a lot. They invite their colleagues to do social things. They are "other-aware" in that they notice when their colleagues are stressed or upset and offer to listen or help. Titles don't matter as much as

PEOPLE BECOME A REFLECTION OF THE ATTITUDES, TRAITS, AND BEHAVIORS THAT LEADERS DISPLAY.

the people who hold the titles. There's a clear decision hierarchy, but all ideas are valued.

This idea of energy within an enterprise is important and has been a focal point of my consulting practice, my research, and my writing. My book *Energized Enterprise* elaborates on the ideas I have introduced here. That book operates on an important premise: that you can find this energy in individuals everywhere. There are some people who are determined to add value and have a good life regardless of what role they hold; they just do what's right and what helps those around them. Even if everyone around them is complaining, they're happy, pleasant, and get the job done. What makes them stand apart are perspective and determination. They've chosen to be that way. They have decided the type of experience they want for themselves and for those around them. Part of being an effective leader is recognizing those individuals who possess such energy and who reflect the values of the enterprise. Then those people must be cultivated and involved in such ways that their energy, like yours, becomes infectious. Be the energy that you wish to see in your organization. Set expectations for what is acceptable. Model a positive attitude and communicate impeccably. It does not take actual superpowers to have people follow in your

BE THE ENERGY THAT YOU WISH TO SEE IN YOUR ORGANIZATION.

footsteps. Like any good superhero, do what is right, what is honest, and you'll begin to notice behaviors such as those listed below throughout your organization.

Some things people do when they are energized include

- smiling and having fun,
- exhibiting excitement about what they need to get done,
- looking forward to going to work and contributing to the mission,
- getting something resolved and moving forward if it is off track,
- talking honestly about what's working and not working in accomplishing their jobs,
- showing connection and alignment with organizational objectives,
- displaying positive behavior even when no one is around to witness it, and
- doing the right thing even if a supervisor is not peeking over their shoulders.

One of the first things I notice in an energized enterprise with effective leadership at the helm is *buzz*. You can feel the buzz. There's a higher pace and energy level. People are much more likely to be proactive to do things ahead of time. They offer ideas. There's speed and proactivity that causes them to make things happen.

They get more results.

To energize others, try this:

1. **LET PEOPLE LEVERAGE THEIR STRENGTHS.** People want to do a great job! For most people, fit is everything. If people are in jobs they think they are not competent to perform or feel they are being underused, then they are going to be miserable, resentful, or both. Put people in the position to utilize their talents and capabilities. (And make certain you are in your best role, as well.)

IF PEOPLE ARE IN JOBS THEY THINK THEY ARE NOT COMPETENT TO PERFORM OR FEEL THEY ARE BEING UNDERUSED, THEN THEY ARE GOING TO BE MISERABLE, RESENTFUL, OR BOTH.

2. **ALLOW PEOPLE TO DO THEIR JOBS.** Don't rob people of the opportunity to excel by taking over their work—that's unmotivating. Do what's best for people, not what's easiest for you. Encourage people to achieve more than what they believe is possible.

Those quickest and most consistent at displaying such traits make for excellent role models and naturally fill the shoes of effective leadership. Find such thinkers and promote them. You probably would not be in the position you are in today—and seeking to continue to develop your abilities by reading this book—if you had not once decided to be one of these people. If you are, I applaud you. If you're still on your way there, it's never too late to examine those parts of your attitude and approach you want to change or improve. You can decide today to become the best version of yourself you are capable of being. Ultimately, we model superhero behavior by choice.

Masterful motivators energize, elevate, and engage by modeling the behaviors they want from their teams. Only when people see their leaders lead by example will they listen to their messages. Effective leaders understand that motivational messages are made up of more than just words; they are *actionable* words, and they expect those they are trying to motivate to react with action as well.

I'll share the thoughts of someone who inspires me to capture what I mean here. Mike Krzyzewski, the legendary men's basketball coach at Duke University, has led the Blue Devils to four NCAA championships and eleven appearances in the Final Four and is viewed by those inside and outside of basketball as a master motivator. In an editorial about his motivational beliefs and techniques for the *Wall Street Journal*, "Coach K" wrote,

> Meaning is understood by seeing a word in action. I ask teams to understand the meaning of dependability by telling them about my

> brother, Bill, who never missed a day of work in thirty-eight years of fighting fires in Chicago. I tell them about willpower by sharing the story of my former player and current associate head coach, Steve Wojciechowski, and his last game on our home court: Wojo only scored one point that day, but his sheer determination led our team to an exciting victory. And I convey the meaning of courage by telling them about my friend and colleague, the late Jim Valvano, who used his own battle with cancer to raise millions of dollars to support cancer research. My hope is that, as the players listen, my brother's example may remind them of the most dependable person in their own lives. Maybe the story of Wojo's senior game will make them think of a moment when they were carried through a tough situation by the strength of their own will. Learning about Jimmy Valvano, they may recall a time when they witnessed true courage. When an audience makes these associations, we have found common ground. We are no longer merely exchanging words; we are being mutually motivated by their meaning.[2]

What can we learn from Krzyzewski's own words? What can we apply from them within our organizations, our "teams"? What actions do we expect from those we lead? What actions do we expect of ourselves? When we're truthful in our words and in the actions they inspire, we create the energized environment that produces satisfaction and productivity.

Leading change relies on improving our own effectiveness while inspiring others and guiding transformation. To do this we become intentional about inspiring our own and others' performance and we find ways to boost morale, satisfaction, and happiness. We bring out the best in others and actively lift others up to support their development. We take the extra minute to pay more attention to people and show them that we care. By strengthening bonds among people, we help them connect to and support the greater good. If we actively look for ways to understand the stress levels of the people around us, it will assist us in understanding their level of motivation. In the end, truly strengthening our motivational mastery comes down to learning new ways to help other people be more effective.

BY STRENGTHENING BONDS AMONG PEOPLE, WE HELP THEM CONNECT TO AND SUPPORT THE GREATER GOOD.

It's up to us to make the decision to care enough about the people we serve to become motivationally masterful. I encourage you to act upon the advice given throughout this chapter, from the smallest acts of reaching out to understand others to the superheroic strength that will come with leveraging their best skills and abilities. If we are sincere in our efforts to motivate others, when they find they work within an environment of support, growth, and energy, they too will find the powers within to soar.

If your LEAP Profile self-assessment indicates you need to boost your motivational mastery, here are some additional action items to keep you on the path to better engaging, elevating, and energizing people within your sphere of influence:

- **ASK MORE QUESTIONS.** You don't always have all the answers, and you won't always have the *best* answer. Ask more questions of your colleagues, and let them offer solutions, too.
- **ABSORB THE STRESS FROM ABOVE.** While it's important to be transparent with your colleagues, people don't need to carry all the emotional burdens from every stakeholder in every project. It can add undue stress to a task, and if you are in a leadership position, it's your job to manage those higher-level stressors without projecting them onto your team.
- **HAVE FUN.** Don't forget to smile, laugh, and create a work environment where people actually want to be.
- **ATTRACT AND RETAIN TOP TALENT.** Recruit top performers who mesh well with your culture. Fitness

for the job isn't enough. Prospective talent should also fit with other employees and with the organization as a whole. Once you have those top players on board, give them something larger than themselves to which they can commit.

- **BE FLEXIBLE.** Different people respond differently to the same kind of management. So, figure out what inspires all the individuals within your team or organization. Realize it takes different skills to manage top performers than it does to manage those who may be struggling.
- **REFLECT.** At the end of every day, ask yourself, "What was the most important thing I did today?" Your answers will help you clarify your purpose, values, and motivations.

MASTERY IN ACTION:
John Travolta, Motivational Superman

It's up to us to let our inner superheroes shine and inspire others to do the same.

Over the years, I've served on the board of directors for several organizations. In fact, I recently completed a two-year term as the board chair of a large charitable organization that helps individuals with disabilities, as well as veterans and their families. Our board was preparing to host our big annual fund-raiser. It's a large production with a full film crew. In attendance are top executives from the federal government, politicians, military leaders, some celebrities, and various dignitaries.

Five days before the event, I received a call to learn that one of our honorees is good friends with John Travolta. John wanted to show up to demonstrate his support at the awards ceremony. I was thrilled because his presence would help us raise more money. The start time for the event was five thirty. Anyone who's going to be onstage arrives early to rehearse. I arrived at three o'clock. After I finished I began to exit the stage. One of the production crew was standing right in front of me. He said, "Hey, you're pretty good!"

Suddenly, I focused and realized it was John Travolta. I asked, "What are you doing here so early?" He smiled and said, "I just flew up from Florida." He said, "I'm ready to work. May I practice?" The production team sprang to life. John added, "I was wondering if I might make a few suggestions that came to mind when I was watching."

John had been sitting in the dark ballroom while I practiced. Very humbly and respectfully, John suggested some changes to camera angles, the mic, the podium, and a few other things. Once the production crew had happily made all of the changes, John practiced his lines. He had a lengthy script that he received the day before.

He practiced a couple times, just like the rest of us. Then he said, "Okay, thank you so much for letting me practice. I feel prepared."

When the awards program began, I went up on stage, delivered my remarks, and John joined me with the presence of a star. He delivered with perfection! Our goal that evening had been to raise close to a million dollars, and we did! The event was wildly successful. When it was over, I was really motivated. It wasn't because John's a celebrity; it was the things that I saw him do that day.

For example, seeing John show up and practice with the rest of us was inspiring. The way he gently made suggestions for improvement to the production crew was so supportive and helpful. By the way, the production chief told me, "I feel awesome. Now my team and I can say we worked with John Travolta."

John chose to show up and support his friend who received the award. John's positive feedback and demonstrated kindness were touching. He connected with hundreds of people by saying, "I feel like I starred in a picture with each and every one of you." John exhibited his motivational superpowers that day by engaging, elevating, and energizing everybody, including me.

BRINGING IT ALL TOGETHER

Here's my takeaway. Every one of us is John Travolta (or Superman or Wonder Woman) to somebody. And, when we acknowledge them, how do they feel? To them, Superman just said, "You're incredible." Or, Wonder Woman just said, "Hey, I see you." That's motivating!

We all have superpowers, and we are all superheroes to someone. How we show up is a choice.

Questions for Reflection, Discovery, and Action

1. In what ways do I actively boost morale, satisfaction, and happiness in my work environment?
2. How do I go about bringing out the best in others and actively lifting them up to support their dreams and their development?
3. Have I created mechanisms to strengthen bonds among people and help them connect to and support the greater good?
4. What actions do I take to understand the stress levels of the people around me?
5. How do I go about understanding the level of motivation of others?
6. What am I willing to do in order to help people around me be more effective?
7. Do I share and demonstrate my own goals with those around me? Do I actively try to inspire others' performances, supporting achievement of individual and collective goals?

8

CREATE YOUR OWN UNIQUE OPPORTUNITIES

Transformational leaders engage in behaviors that are bold, creative, and powerful. These behaviors include asking questions, seeking and providing feedback, taking risks, managing physical and mental health, providing direction, and recognizing others' hard work. Consistently exhibiting such behaviors sets a standard, and people align themselves with the high levels of performance that become evident from the result of these behaviors. People emulate the behaviors they see leaders exhibiting. Whether leaders realize it or not, their behaviors, and even their attitudes, are contagious.

My team at TSI encourages our clients to experiment with and model transformational leadership behaviors in order to become more effective and to ultimately help their workforces achieve bolder goals. We coach and mentor leaders—like Diana, a senior executive of a multibillion-dollar enterprise—to unleash their inner superheroes, even if it means taking a risk from time to time. We've found that these behaviors often become contagious throughout the organization. Diana took on this challenge with gusto. She and her organization offer a wonderful example of transformational leadership.

TRANSFORMATIONAL LEADERS ENGAGE IN BEHAVIORS THAT APPEAR BOLD, CREATIVE, AND POWERFUL.

When we first started working with Diana, the top one hundred leaders of her organization were functioning independently in their stovepipes without sharing important information. This lack of collaboration felt right to them, because the organization was so big and spread out. They only met every six months, and during those biannual meetings they spent their time complaining. Diana's top twenty leaders basically did the same thing. This process was not working at all, and she knew it.

We suggested that Diana ramp up slowly to boost the interaction among her senior leaders over time, so they would eventually collaborate more regularly to align their messaging and priorities across the whole enterprise. The first step was to invite the top one hundred leaders to Diana's smaller, twenty-person, inner-circle meetings. She also changed the frequency of these meetings from biannual to quarterly. These changes gave them quality time together to think strategically every three months.

We also helped Diana recognize that strategic decisions weren't being implemented. We suggested thirty-minute stand-up meetings with her top twenty team members to hold their feet to the fire about implementation. After about a year, Diana ramped up the frequency of the quarterly meetings so that they occurred every month. These monthly gatherings enabled her and her team of a hundred to begin examining the entire portfolio that their enterprise delivers. These meetings also allowed them to build deeper rapport with one another and to take the time they needed to analyze problems.

We have found that in many cases, when people are so frozen and risk averse, it's heretical for them to think about taking risks that might fail. To unfreeze her people, Diana first introduced the idea of bold moves that involve risk-taking, and she started talking about it regularly. Now her top leaders are sharing this idea with their people and encouraging them to take risks that could ultimately lead to improvement. Second, Diana began to communicate an intense focus on speed to affordable capability. Her theme is, "How fast can we get something they can afford in the hands of our customers who need it?" Third, Diana began using more humor when holding people accountable in group settings, using honey, not vinegar. For example, she will ask with a smile and a twinkle in her eye, "Can't you cut that cycle time in half?" Everyone chuckles, including the recipient of the question, and it makes the situation less tense. However, everyone still knows Diana is intent on reducing cycle time.

Another thing we suggested was that Diana share a "decoder ring" document to describe herself, her preferences, her irritants, and her expectations. Her team found this to be very useful and said that it helped them to improve their individual relationships with her. Many of them then shared the same type of document with their teams and found that more of their relationships improved. It's great to see basic psychology principles such as this make a difference in people's professional lives.

Within Diana's team of one hundred leaders, there was diversity of gender, ethnicity, experience, and background, but no age diversity. Everyone was over fifty years old. We recommended inviting interns into her monthly meetings so that the younger workforce could begin getting exposure to these strategic conversations. Then, we helped launch a program called reverse mentoring where young professionals would come in and shadow Diana for two weeks at a time, then offer her feedback on how young professionals across the enterprise would likely react to what she does and says. Another thing Diana has done is package her priorities into easy-to-understand, alliterative language such as the tag line "Commit, Collaborate, Care, and Celebrate."

We also coached Diana to try some new behaviors on the communication front, which resulted in a more aligned workforce as people came to better understand her approach and the mission of the enterprise. For example, she began sending her team a weekly email called "Back to Basics" about topics such as teamwork, leadership, and motivation. She would bring bagels for breakfast every Friday morning, and she and her team of direct reports would discuss those topics. In addition, Diana launched a constant messaging campaign plan including a strong presence on social media, regular all-hands emails, and public-speaking events, both internal and external, almost every day.

Diana regularly encourages everyone within her sphere of influence to reach inside themselves to unleash their inner superpowers and to help their teams do the same. Recently, we interviewed some of Diana's colleagues and asked them if they had unleashed any dormant superpowers as a result of Diana setting an example and being so supportive of them. Everyone said yes. A few superpowers they say are now unleashed within the organization include the following:

- Analyzing all viewpoints
- Anticipating what customers want
- Applying whatever the rules are
- Asking others for help
- Being a good diplomat
- Being a servant leader
- Being humble
- Being open minded
- Building happy teams
- Building relationship bridges
- Communicating masterfully
- Demonstrating inclusiveness
- Finding win-wins
- Getting people to come together
- Giving great presentations
- Giving people reinforcement
- Helping natural leaders to excel
- Helping all see what's important
- Helping people understand "why"
- Integrating information
- Keeping emotions in check

- Knowing people's true colors
- Leading with intention
- Learning from others' experiences
- Lifting people up
- Liking everyone; showing caring
- Listening with compassion
- Loving people
- Ensuring everyone understands
- Managing priorities
- Organizing chaos
- Pulling the right teams together
- Seeing performance gaps
- Showing gratitude and kindness
- Showing creativity
- Simplifying things
- Supporting our workplace culture
- Taking initiative
- Talking to everybody
- Telling really good stories
- Trusting intuition
- Working to do the right thing

Wow, this sounds like a great place to work! Now, we joke with Diana that since she has revealed her inner superhero and unleashed so much potential throughout her workforce, perhaps she should start calling herself Wonder Woman.

Diana's example could best be labeled a case study in contagious transformation. She demonstrated the kind of bold, creative, and powerful behaviors that made her people wish to align themselves with the high levels of performance they wished to emulate.

SUPERHERO ESSENTIALS

People like Diana who achieve meaningful success do three things. They

- imagine, create, and innovate where others don't;
- manage stress, time, and data; and
- encourage, inspire, and mentor others.

These three essentials will help you to energize yourself and others. Another way to think about them is that they are preliminary suppositions to effective leadership.

Imagination, Creativity, and Innovation Create Opportunities

Imagination is the ability and process of inventing scenarios within the mind from perceiving the world around us. Effective individuals create supportive environments that encourage everyone to use their imaginations to create new possibilities.

Creativity is the process of producing something that is both original and worthwhile. It's a phenomenon whereby something new and valuable is generated. Effective people choose to fan the flames of creativity throughout their spheres of influence.

Innovation is about applying new, original solutions in new ways. Effective people not only promote innovation, they recognize and reward it in others.

One of the greatest powers in the history of humankind has been humans' creative nature, our ability to imagine possibilities and take innovative strides. Creativity is the foundation of our culture. Your future is limitless if your full potential is unleashed and you operate at full capacity.

People Respect Those Who Manage Stress, Time, and Data

Despite difficult pressures, effective people remain focused, clear, and calm, which builds the confidence of everyone around them. Due to the natural "fight-or-flight" response, certain instincts take over when people respond to stress. The faster we can identify our fight-or-flight response and avoid pumping unneeded adrenaline through our body, the more easily we can respond to the situation and to the people at hand.

WE MUST BE ABLE TO OVERRIDE INSTINCT IN STRESSFUL WORK SETTINGS OR WE'LL END UP FEEDING TENSION AND FUELING REACTIVE RESPONSES.

As successful and influential people, we must be able to override instinct in stressful work settings or we'll end up feeding tension and fueling reactive responses. We can model for others how to choose tools to reduce psychological stress. In fact, studies show that people who choose to meet stressors with a positive attitude develop a remarkable hardiness that allows them to stay committed, feel in control, and seek challenges. This hardiness is important for a healthy culture.

THROUGH THE LENS OF SCIENCE:
Developing Grit

The hardiness required by a healthy culture and the positive attitude necessary to develop it are discussed at length within David G. Myers and C. Nathan DeWall's book *Psychology*. In it, they show that having a sense of control, developing more optimistic thinking, and building social support can help us experience less stress and thus improve our health. Moreover, these factors interrelate: people who have been upbeat about themselves and their future have tended also to enjoy health-promoting social ties, according to findings by Fredrick Stinson and his colleagues.

Moreover—and this is one of psychology's most consistent findings—happiness doesn't just feel good; it *does* good. In study after study, a mood-boosting experience (finding money, succeeding on a challenging task, recalling a happy event) has made people more likely to give money, pick up someone's dropped papers, volunteer time, and do other good deeds. Psychologists call it the "feel-good, do-good phenomenon," say Myers and DeWall, citing a1990 study by Peter Salovey. When combined with a positive enthusiasm, sustained effort predicts success. Angela Duckworth and Martin Seligman have a name for this passionate dedication to an ambitious, long-term goal: *grit*. Achievement involves much more than raw ability. That is why organizational psychologists seek ways to train employees to exhibit resilience under stress.

Being successful takes time, but time is not the enemy of successful people. Instead, it's a precious resource to be managed as carefully as any project. While we should be conscientious with our time and the time of others, we need enough of it to do things right. Time should be managed with care, especially when we are committed to offsetting stress. The best way to use limited time is to become more efficient. Efficiency is a choice; more accurately, efficiency is a collection of hundreds of minor choices about how we behave from day to day.

For example, I was taught by a professional organizer to lay out everything I would need for the next day the night before. I learned that by preparing myself by setting out my coffee, clothing, work supplies, and keys, I could do everything twice as fast—and it helped me to not forget important things I used to forget in my morning rush.

Efficiency depends on a moment-to-moment conscious evolution in our behavior concerning time. And, our time-management skills have a far-reaching collateral impact. By consciously respecting the use of time, we are treating those around us as the precious resources they are. Time management is about respect for others, and effectively managing time boosts others' impressions of us.

Effective time management puts into action our commitment to ensure there is enough time, for example, to frame the right questions and get good answers, to walk around and listen, and to be open to new ideas. Time management is especially important in hectic environments.

Encouragement, Inspiration, and Mentoring Help Us Flourish

Another way to soar is to get everyone involved in our endeavors. Start encouraging folks to achieve more than what they think is possible. Make it your mission to inspire people to question their assumptions, think for themselves, reframe problems, and approach matters in innovative, collaborative ways. Experiment with paying focused attention to people's personal needs for achievement and development. Take responsibility when things go wrong. When great things happen, go ahead and give others the credit.

Act as a caring, compassionate, and empathetic mentor. Think, speak, and act from the heart as a catalyst for results. For example, we grow when we adopt the mind-set of not always trying to be right but giving up some of our ego to encourage and grow relationships that work for all. The old marriage truism still holds: Do you want to be right, or do you want a relationship? Giving more of ourselves to empower others is inspiring. When we are doing our best, it inspires the people around us to do their best.

THROUGH THE LENS OF SCIENCE:
Necessary Empathy

Research detailed in the journal *Science* found the most successful groups or teams were those in which the participants found empathy with one another. The issue of psychological safety is viewed by Google as a key to successful teams and offers a great example of how cultivating empathy in a corporate setting can be transformational:

> The behaviors that create psychological safety—conversational turn-taking and empathy—are part of the same unwritten rules we often turn to, as individuals, when we need to establish a bond. And those human bonds matter as much at work as anywhere else. In fact, they sometimes matter more.[1]

LEADERSHIP RULES THAT WILL HELP YOU SOAR

Successful people use tools to help guide their paths. On your personal and professional path, I suggest you consider using a set of rules for transformational leaders. I label these as "rules," because I believe they are so important for effective leadership that I live by them. They are strategies so powerful that you will witness their effect on your life and on the impact such transformation will have on those around you. These rules enhance emotional intelligence, which *Psychology Today* defines as "the ability to identify and manage one's own emotions, as well as the emotions of others." Such rules are based on learning, growing, and risk-taking. The rules promote taking responsibility for one's self and one's relationships and endeavors. And they are based on holding oneself accountable at the highest level. I encourage you to turn to them in all you do.

The rules that follow, like the essentials on which they are built, help you show people that you care about them and help you to make every thought, word, and deed count. These rules help you to elevate others by creating connections with people, linking them with one another, and helping them to be their very best. Over the past twenty-five years, after being introduced to them by one of our mentors, my colleagues and I have applied these rules to help thousands of people in many organizations be more effective.

1. Maintain a Supportive Environment

Recognize, encourage, and help people who take risks. If people want to try a new way of doing things, give them the chance to try it; and if they succeed, recognize their success. If the new way fails, celebrate the lesson learned, encourage them to keep looking for ways to do things better, and evaluate what is worth retaining from the old way *and* from the experiment. Really listen to what others are saying. Ask questions to clarify anything that you don't fully understand. Read the person's body language and respond appropriately. If the person looks hurt, ask if he or she feels bad about something and would like to talk about it. Invite people to participate; including and involving people is one true mark of a leader. To make such involvement an active practice, engage others by opening up meetings to more people whenever appropriate; pull people into conversations and learn their thoughts. Taking actions like these to build a supportive environment will improve your organization's culture.

For example, sharing failure can be supportive and bring a group together. Remembering our epic failures and cringeworthy moments—once we get past the initial pain and embarrassment and the lessons learned—that's where the laughter is, in the connection and the community that will emerge and where we find the shared human experience and vitality.

I've certainly had to learn such lessons the hard way. Several years ago, the leadership team at TSI launched an initiative to productize some of our solutions. In an attempt to scale our business and serve more customers, we embarked on an effort to package a subset of our services. We held several strategy meetings to determine what the scope would look like, and we had fun brainstorming catchy names. However, at that same time, we were kicking off work on several new contracts, and we became distracted from the task of scaling the business. We mistakenly tabled the productization effort as we were swept up in managing our business and working with clients. A short time later, sequestration, a package of automatic government spending cuts, was triggered when legislators did not come to an agreement on a deficit-reduction package. Federal funds to buy products and services decreased substantially, hitting our industry hard. Contracting firms struggled to keep their doors open. These spending cuts changed the way the government bought services, and had we fully executed our efforts to productize, we would have been in a stronger position as a company during that difficult time. Due to factors and processes unique to the government-contracting industry, having a packaged service would have given many of our customers a way to contract with us during that time. We weathered the storm but missed an opportunity and lost momentum. Had we executed on the vision we had for productization and stayed the course on this strategic initiative despite the demands of everyday work, we would have been positioned differently. It took a while to make up for lost time. We made the mistake of losing sight of the bigger picture and strategic priorities for a moment due to daily demands, and we paid the price of missed opportunity and growth.

A struggle to be perfect can bring respect. However,

celebrating wins *and* admitting losses can open hearts. Never miss the opportunity for empathy, for recognizing common ground, and for learning from mistakes.

2. Maintain Confidentiality

Weigh carefully the potential consequences of quoting coworkers and spreading gossip. This means guarding against attribution and retribution. First, attributing statements to others out of context can be misleading. If they want to share something about the meeting with those who were not in attendance, ask them to keep it general without pointing any fingers at individuals. Second, remember that people who receive retribution for what they do or say will be shy about taking the lead or sharing their opinions in the future. As you encourage people to share their opinions and provide input, be careful not to punish them in any way after the fact if you don't agree with their suggestions or point of view. Maintaining confidentiality by guarding against attribution and retribution builds trust and puts people at ease to be creative. Breaking confidentiality weakens trust and promotes fear and bad feelings. The choice is ours to create a culture of trust with the help of this leadership rule.

3. Stay Focused and Be Prepared

Define and understand what it means to be on task and how to remain there. It's easy to get distracted and discouraged by the million things in your life. But the way to really make things happen and achieve your goals is to clear your mind, pull together the tools you need, and fully embrace the situation at hand. For example, make sure you get enough sleep and that you aren't overscheduling yourself to the point that you can't pay attention. And, don't hold the kinds of expectations that result in people being sleepy, overbooked, and unable to show up rested and alert at all times. Every leader can do little things like this to ensure that he or she shows up 100 percent in the moment and that all members of the organization realize that they, too, are expected and encouraged to arrive fully engaged.

AS YOU ENCOURAGE PEOPLE TO SHARE THEIR OPINIONS AND PROVIDE INPUT, BE CAREFUL NOT TO PUNISH THEM IN ANY WAY AFTER THE FACT IF YOU DON'T AGREE WITH THEIR SUGGESTIONS OR POINT OF VIEW.

4. Manage All Agreements

Your cumulative record of adherence to your commitments forms the essence of how others view you. Prioritize your commitments, make fewer of them, and keep the ones that you make. Seek to minimize the impact of any obligations that circumstances force you to break by informing others well in advance. If this is not possible, acknowledge your inability to maintain a commitment as soon as possible after the fact. One example of an important agreement is time. How you manage scheduling time with your team is very important. If you set a meeting to start at nine o'clock and you show up at a quarter past nine, what message does that send to those in attendance? Beyond time, extend this type of management to every one of your agreements to build trust with everyone you know. As leaders, it's our responsibility to set a great example of managing all agreements, especially with respect to time. People notice our behaviors and follow our lead.

YOUR CUMULATIVE RECORD OF ADHERENCE TO YOUR COMMITMENTS FORMS THE ESSENCE OF HOW OTHERS VIEW YOU.

5. Use Open, Honest, and Direct Communication

Practice being open: be clear as opposed to sending hidden messages. If a person walks away from a conversation with you and asks, "What was he trying to tell me?" the whole conversation was a waste of time. Practice being honest: truthfully share your thoughts, ideas, and feelings. Although stretching the truth or telling a little white lie may be convenient, keeping track of untruths is distracting and can cause leaders to lose focus. Practice being direct: share your message with the person it is intended for as opposed to telling someone you hope will pass it along. What's the point of telling everyone else what you really need to tell a particular individual? It's inefficient, and you run the risk of your message being transmitted incorrectly. As leaders, it's our job to be role models for impeccable communication, and others will be influenced to do the same.

6. Hold a Proper Attitude for Learning

Remain open to, contribute to, and build upon new ideas. No matter what is said, remain open to the possibility that all ideas have value and that you can learn from them. Suspend judgment, seeking first to understand the message of the other person. Learning is not confined to childhood or to school but takes place throughout life and in a range of situations. Being open to the possibility of learning from everyone enhances social inclusion, active participation, and professional development. Effective leaders constantly seek to learn new things and encounter alternative beliefs, cultures, and values. When leaders stop doing this, their personal development stops, too.

Embrace every opportunity you have to learn from others. This doesn't mean agreeing with them on everything. We can learn from many people with whom we have nothing in common. Learning from others helps us grow emotionally, keeps us from making mistakes, and can often help with our own decision-making. The beauty of wanting to learn from others is that you will remain open and willing to listen, which, in return, will draw others toward you. This will also open many new doors and experiences. Not only that, maintaining a proper attitude for learning can make us effective teachers. So, as well as learning from the experiences of others, we may also discover a great demand by people who want to learn from us.

EMBRACE EVERY OPPORTUNITY YOU HAVE TO LEARN FROM OTHERS.

7. Be Self-Monitoring

View your behaviors and see how they play out. Continuously hold up the mirror to see your reflection. Then, make appropriate adjustments. This leadership rule is your reminder to continuously build your self-awareness. It is also your reminder to monitor your adherence to the other six leadership rules. To practice self-monitoring, pretend you're holding up a video camera and capturing your every thought, word, and deed. Pretend to play it back and watch yourself in action. Are you effectively communicating with people, supporting them, staying focused?

If so, great! If not, you can choose new thoughts, words, and deeds. Or take this advice literally and occasionally have yourself filmed, unobtrusively, when conducting a meeting or delivering a presentation.

These leadership rules, when put into action, help guide behaviors and attitudes that will keep us performing our best and will inspire those around us to do the same. Tools like the leadership rules elevate us and maximize our ability to make a meaningful difference. Follow them diligently, and you might even come to be seen as a superhero by the people you work with and care about.

BRINGING IT ALL TOGETHER

Ideally, every one of us would be our best, do great things, and put into motion the essentials and rules for success on a daily basis. Doing so would seem the most natural thing. Wouldn't taking such action be wonderful? Yes! But, as I've said, our comfort zones can hold us back. So, sometimes we must make uncomfortable choices to take charge of our lives and be focused on achieving our dreams. We must believe there is something extraordinary inside of us.

Every individual can be transformed from being complacent with the status quo to embracing all that life has to offer. There is a proven solution—becoming agile—for tending to our spirits, cultivating our minds, and making our results more productively fruitful. Becoming agile involves nurturing and growing our life force. Science and industry abound with research and results of how agile people who are also personally, interpersonally, organizationally, and motivationally masterful can propel themselves to new heights. Yes, you can make such a choice and apply this wisdom to transform yourself. You can choose to develop your superhero powers, take the leap, and soar.

Questions for Reflection, Discovery, and Action

1. What actions am I taking to maintain a supportive environment at home and at work for myself and for others? What else can I do?
2. What behaviors do I exhibit to maintain confidentiality? What else can I do?
3. What steps do I take in order to be focused and prepared? What else can I do?
4. What actions do I take to help me manage my agreements? What else can I do?
5. What do I do to ensure that I'm open, honest, and direct? What else can I do?
6. How do I demonstrate that I value learning? What else can I do?
7. What are the ways I put self-monitoring in motion? What else can I do?

9

UNLEASH YOUR INNER SUPERHERO AND SOAR

When I attended the University of Tennessee as an undergraduate, Pat Summitt was the women's basketball coach. One of the most successful coaches of all time, Summitt led the University of Tennessee women's basketball team to 1,098 wins and eight national championships. She served as head coach for thirty years. During my time at Tennessee, Summitt also guided the US women's national team to an Olympic gold medal. As a result, I can't begin to describe, as a young woman, how proud I was to be a Tennessee Vol. Over thirty-eight years, she coached a diverse team, giving them one common goal and the steps and inspiration to achieve it.

Writing at the time of Summitt's death and the end of her battle with Alzheimer's, and recalling when he had awarded her the Presidential Medal of Freedom in 2012, President Barack Obama said,

> Nobody walked off a college basketball court victorious more times than Tennessee's Pat Summitt. For four decades, she outworked her rivals, made winning an attitude, loved her players like family, and became a role model to millions of Americans, including our two daughters.[1]

I was never an athlete. However, a few years ago, inspired in part by Coach Summitt, I decided to give myself some physical challenges and seek out new fitness experiences. I challenged myself to step out of my comfort zone and try something beyond my normal fitness routine. I started Pilates, which was new and different for me. But I decided to be curious about Pilates and open my mind to try it. Pretty soon Pilates led to flying trapeze, and trapeze led to aerial yoga. (I guess I took the "soar" element of my belief system quite literally.) Being active, taking personal risks, finding joy in the unknown, all of the elements of my personal philosophy are inextricably interwoven with the energy and attitude I bring into the office and to the podium.

I don't think I've suddenly discovered superhero powers and can actually fly, but some days it feels close. My choice to make a change in my life is one example of the kind of conscious evolution we can pursue in our quest to become more masterful.

Now it's time to put your own dreams in motion, time to apply what you've learned from the ideas, examples, and research you have encountered in this book and exponentially magnify your leadership impact. You'll boost your untapped potential to reach new crests of performance. You can quickly and practically put the tools and techniques from this book into action and apply the results to form your own evolving success story. These techniques are used by effective people from every walk of life. Success with these methods requires that you imagine new possibilities and commit to improving your performance. Let's review some key concepts that you can apply now.

TRANSFORMATION REQUIRES A SHIFT IN PERSPECTIVE AND VISION

I imagine that you want to unleash a positive dynamic within your life as you realize a better you and become a source of genuine inspiration. Great! But, ultimately, transformation is about a mindful and conscious shift in perspective and action. We can't just *say* we're going to be successful and turn to a quick-fix program. We're not discussing a fad diet or forgettable buzz term bandied about at this year's iteration of an annual conference. The changes this book suggests require continual commitment and conscious effort. A shift in perspective must rely upon a powerful vision that includes attending to your growth. Throughout this book I've encouraged you to take yourself to the next level of effectiveness. It's up to you to shift your perspective, enhance your vision, and enroll others to help you achieve your transformation.

TRANSFORMATION IS ABOUT A MINDFUL AND CONSCIOUS SHIFT IN PERSPECTIVE AND ACTION. WE CAN'T JUST SAY WE'RE GOING TO BE SUCCESSFUL AND TURN TO A QUICK-FIX PROGRAM.

RESULTS REQUIRE COMMITMENT

If you are committed to going beyond your own current limits and want the most for yourself and others, you have the choice to make it happen. It involves demonstrating the kind of daily commitment my parents did to elevate their lives and lead us into a future of their own making. And remember, challenging ourselves and others to experiment with new behaviors is part of being effective. By committing to adjust our sentiment and mind-set, we can fulfill our vision and achieve new heights. As we become more masterful, we can apply corrective strategies, close critical gaps, and evaluate our desired results. We can conquer how to think and feel in new ways that make a positive difference for ourselves and those around us. As you adjust your mind-set, I challenge you to go beyond your current capabilities and convince others to push their limits. You can achieve this, and I predict you will find it fulfilling.

Effectiveness starts with pushing yourself to become more aware of your strengths, weaknesses, and capabilities. Effectiveness means maintaining and managing your courage, clarity, power, and physical limitations in a way that promotes improvement, civility, and wisdom within yourself and your endeavors. It means following role models like my father, who chose to help others and consistently demonstrate courage. And it also means serving as a role model for others to follow while they commit to something bigger than themselves.

When we live with purpose, build strong relationships, understand our environment, and are motivated to succeed, our lives become vibrant. I encourage you to think about living your best life, and then take actions to make it a reality. I advise you to contemplate the essence of relationships, and take steps to improve these bonds. Also, I suggest you look for ways to become more situationally aware of the systems within which you reside. Finally, I implore you to consider the meaning of motivation, and then get in motion to boost it for everyone in your reach.

FOUR THINGS TO CONSIDER BEFORE YOU ACT

Before you set forth to apply the tools and techniques that I've shared with you, I invite you to contemplate and embrace some important characteristics of effective people: attributes, choices, signs, and results. These are good benchmarks for those who choose to transform their lives. It's really up to each one of us to exhibit great attributes, make sound choices, manifest signs of success, and create bold results.

1. Attributes of Effective People

A positive change in improving our effectiveness relies on inspiring, modeling, driving, and guiding change around us. Some attributes to consider adopting include self-awareness, heart, sensitivity, and persuasiveness.

- **SELF-AWARENESS**. People are drawn to individuals who are self-aware, and those individuals have a confidence that warrants the trust others place in them. We can build our self-awareness by asking others for their insights on what we don't know about ourselves. This helps us become more effective, both personally and professionally.

- **HEART.** Transformation happens in our hearts and in our habits. Otherwise, change will be superficial, and old habits will slip back into place when the pressure is high—just when a new and better way of working is most important. Being in touch with people is not just a nice idea; it is crucial to the daily function of our lives. Connectedness enables us to capture the hearts and minds of others. As I've said before in this book, but repeat here because it is so accurate, people don't care what we know until they know that we care.

TRANSFORMATION HAPPENS IN OUR HEARTS AND IN OUR HABITS. OTHERWISE, CHANGE WILL BE SUPERFICIAL.

- **SENSITIVITY.** Effective individuals can read people, and they realize that it's imperative to listen and see things from other folks' points of view. Listening is only a start. Being aware of the values and emotions of others is crucial for wielding influence. To have a positive impact on others, we first sense how people feel and then understand their position. This requires our vigilance and conscious flexibility to respond in real time to feedback and to exercise social competence. To respond effectively to the people in our work environment, we cultivate an awareness of what is important to them.

- **PERSUASIVENESS.** Effective people convince others to help them. This kind of persuasion requires engaging people's hearts and minds and doing so with sincerity. As essential steps in influencing others, take the time to establish bonds, collaborate, and be patient.

2. Choices of Effective People

Effective people have great resilience and vision. This is a result of choosing to focus our hearts and minds on adopting a discipline that will energize people and help them do more than just work hard. Our discipline helps others go above and beyond with common direction, energy, vitality, harmony, and spirit. What follows are some choices we can make as part of adopting a stronger discipline.

- **BUILD YOUR RELATIONSHIPS.** Effective people build relationships, and relationships are the core of their networks. New and maturing bonds expand those networks. Individuals who choose to build bonds naturally cultivate and maintain extensive informal networks. Seek out relationships that are mutually beneficial, and then build rapport. Choose to be less protective of your own time and agenda, and accept more requests to work cooperatively with others. It's all a balancing act, and I encourage you to balance your own critical work with helping others as you build accounts of goodwill with people across your sphere of influence.

- **UNITE PEOPLE AND IDEAS.** Make your vision a shared goal. By engaging the hearts of everyone as we work together to lead a transformation, we can prepare others to share in accomplishments, which would not be possible if all or most of them were not motivated by a sense of connection to something bigger. When people are connected to something bigger, they want to be better colleagues, helpers, and mentors. They strive to become leaders themselves. Developing and attaining shared goals results in real, lasting transformation that leads to greater levels of performance.
- **LEVERAGE YOUR NETWORKS.** Effective people build networks. Strong networks require trust. Networks that you build on trust can be the most supportive allies in your efforts to lead yourself and others to greatness. There are many advantages to having well-developed networks. People who leverage their networks have an immense time advantage over those who have to use broader, more general sources of information to find answers. As I've discussed at greater length in *Leaders in Motion, Everybody's Business,* and *Energized Enterprise*, it's estimated that for every hour a well-connected individual spends

seeking answers through a network, the average person would spend several hours gathering the same information. Our networks can also help us influence others, because our endorsements from people within our spheres of influence create added support and credibility for our ideas.

A network of contacts is crucial personal capital. Among effective leaders, what benefits the individual also benefits the group. The network of contacts we choose creates a wealth of knowledge, support, and goodwill that we bring to everyone around us. Build good bonds throughout your career and build a leadership network full of people outside of your daily circles who can contribute to a variety of your bold goals and enhance your success story.

3. Signs of Effective People

Effective people plant and cultivate seeds of energy. They have a high level of self-confidence. They're awake, alive, alert, and open to what is going on in the world.

We can find this energy in people everywhere. We meet them all the time, and we can see they have it. We can choose to find the people who are already awake and help them get brighter and shinier. So, be the energy that you wish to see around you. Model a positive attitude and communicate impeccably. People will follow in your footsteps, and you'll notice the signs.

There are some people who are determined to add value and have a good life regardless of what life, work, and other people hand them. Even if everyone around them is complaining, they're happy, pleasant, and get the job done. What makes them stand apart is perspective and determination. They've chosen to be that way. They have decided the type of experience they want for themselves and for those around them. These people are excellent role models and naturally fill the shoes of effective leadership. You may have decided to be one of these people. If so, I applaud you. If not, it's never too late to change.

4. Results of Effective People

We can bring our lives into balance by making small investments that yield big returns in happiness, productivity, effectiveness, and innovation. By implementing the guidance I've laid out, you can achieve three things that I assert are critical to success and influence in life and work. You can:

- successfully use clearly stated goals and focus your efforts to improve performance and let everyone know what you seek to accomplish,
- effectively measure and analyze performance to find which actions work and deserve further investment

as well as which need to be fixed or stopped, and

- initiate frequent progress reviews on your goals to monitor trends and identify actions likely to increase performance.

By putting this guidance in motion, your life will change. How? You will have put yourself in environments where people frequently smile, exhibit happiness, and show an abundance of energy. Why will this have happened? What will have driven this transformation? You will have driven it as an individual who has advanced to the leading edge by becoming more personally, interpersonally, organizationally, and motivationally masterful.

SOARING TO NEW HEIGHTS

Soaring to new heights is something we can all do. We can expedite the rate at which we become more masterful by investing wisely in education, training, and development. My assertion: make daily decisions to boost your Leadership Effectiveness And Potential, and consciously surround yourself with people who exhibit the same drive. Then, do everything you can to further develop and leverage this strength. In the end, when it comes to developing as a leader, we must behave as though every *thought*, *word*, and *deed* counts.

I understand the value of such actions, in large part because I was graced with mentors who embodied them: my parents. My parents embodied a commitment to achieving their dreams while maintaining their values and a devotion to others in their lives. And the energy with which they pursued their goals on their family's behalf became guiding lights, as I began to venture out to find my own way in the world. Their patience and calmness as they shepherded my siblings and me through our ongoing family transformation became my own, and the compassion that they lived inspired the same in me.

Transformational opportunities are important sustenance, but not all goals are created equally. For example, my frugal parents did not own a phone until purchasing one when I was about twelve years old. Until that time, I had pined for the chance to call and talk to my friends the way I heard about them calling and talking to one another. Getting a phone seemed, to me, like a priority goal—until we got one. After calling my best friend every day after school to talk about boys and to exchange other gossip for six months straight, I realized that we had really been fine without the phone and its tiresome drain on my energy. The phone had only been a possession. And, for me, it did not lead to fulfillment. Today, as a leader, I am careful to focus on goals that are not based on things or money but instead are aimed at making a positive difference in the quality of employees' and clients' lives.

This is but one of any number of lessons I gained from closely observing how my parents conducted themselves and how they demonstrated what they valued. I shared with you some of their other important lessons early in the book. What they demonstrated echoes what I found in the people at the center of the "Mastery in Action" sections you have read as well. Together they form the bedrock of my beliefs about leadership and transformation. From such examples we can all find models of excellence.

BRINGING IT ALL TOGETHER

Your life can become a colorful landscape of positive results as a result of boosting your agility to soar higher. Today, you have an opportunity to access and expand the untapped potential in yourself to reach higher crests of performance. As a result, I envision a day when you could be sought out by science and industry as an expert in individual effectiveness.

In the future, we can thrive in this complex world as soaring, effective people and sow the seeds of a new beginning within our spheres of influence. In fact, I can envision us helping others to blossom and flourish as we adopt a discipline to help everyone, including ourselves, to soar—making our lives, the lives of those around us, and our workplaces fulfilling and invigorating. Now is the time for us to believe we have extraordinary powers inside ourselves and draw upon them. What's the role of any superhero? To help others.

Questions for Reflection, Discovery, and Action

1. Am I practicing kindness every day?
2. Do I ask others how they're doing or "how their world is today" and then take the time to really *listen* to their answers?
3. Am I someone others can confide in without reproach?
4. Do I ask my colleagues how I can help them today?
5. Do I propose social gatherings, and are my suggestions inclusive and doable for people?
6. Have I thought about simply asking a colleague or friend, "How do you think I could have handled this situation differently?"
7. How can I use humor to diffuse a potential conflict, while being careful not to insult the individuals involved?
8. What actions, however small, can I take to make someone else's day a bit brighter and thus build our longer-term relationship?
9. What special skill or talent do I have that can help a friend with a difficulty he or she is having? What is stopping me from doing so?

LEADERSHIP LIBRARY

Boost personal and interpersonal mastery with ***Leaders in Motion: Winning the Race for Organizational Health, Wealth, and Creative Power***

Expand and strengthen organizational mastery with ***Everybody's Business: Engaging Your Total Enterprise to Boost Quality, Speed, Savings and Innovation***

Develop and magnify motivational mastery with ***Energized Enterprise: Leading Your Workforce to New Peaks of Performance in the Public Sector and Beyond***

Expand results, leverage relationships, integrate your environment, and inspire performance with ***LEAP: Master Your Superpowers, Soar to the Leading Edge***

WHY LEAP?

DISCOVERY AND INSIGHT

Leadership Effectiveness and Potential (LEAP) is an assessment framework to identify strengths and developmental opportunities to become more personally, interpersonally, organizationally, and motivationally agile.

The LEAP suite of assessments includes:

- LEAP Enterprise: Learn to measure perceptions across entire organizations
- LEAP Profile: Designed for individual awareness and development
- LEAP 360 Degree Feedback: Help leaders seek and receive feedback

KNOWLEDGE AND GROWTH

LEAP instructs with group and team training. LEAP workshops explore how to put in motion the latest research and philosophy on motivating and energizing the workforce. The workshop format combines experiential learning, paired mentoring, group discussions, individual development, and action planning.

MOTIVATION AND EVOLUTION

LEAP guides leaders with coaching and mentoring. The LEAP team of workplace psychologists and certified coaches helps executives, managers, and leaders heighten their awareness of what it takes to be their best, do great things, and have meaningful success. We use a proven process that illuminates a path of evolution and growth for both emerging and experienced leaders within your organization.

The LEAP App is packed with coaching tips and action items to take performance to the next level. This valuable tool can be used as a stand-alone self-coaching toolkit, or as a supplement to coaching.

PERFORMANCE AND RESULTS

Does your organization need to boost quality, speed, savings, or innovation? LEAP consultants help leaders fine-tune performance and achieve their goals for improvement and transformation. Our PATH PLANNING and QUICK METRICS assist leaders in navigating the road to tangible results.

- Maximize Leadership Effectiveness and Potential
- Boost effectiveness
- Increase alignment
- Improve relationships
- Strengthen collaboration
- Magnify total systems thinking
- Amplify emotional intelligence
- Enhance clarity of growth areas
- Accelerate development

THE LEAP APP

The LEAP app is your pocket coach to help you be your best, do great things, and have meaningful success. LEAP, or Leadership Effectiveness And Potential, is a powerful framework for boosting your current strengths and seizing exciting growth opportunities. The LEAP app mentors you to become more personally, interpersonally, organizationally, and motivationally masterful.

Let the LEAP app guide you to expand your results, leverage your relationships, integrate your environment, and inspire great performance. Use the LEAP app to assess your superpowers, experiment with new behaviors, and achieve your boldest goals. Make the leap today!

Features:

- Take the LEAP Profile to assess yourself and make decisions for your growth.
- View a dynamic display of assessment results that support your development.
- Track your personalized history of assessment results to monitor your progress.
- Receive actionable tips to help you advance to your leading edge of performance.
- Gain skills and information to soar to new heights personally and professionally.
- View videos on personal, interpersonal, organizational, and motivational mastery.

WWW.THELEAPAPP.COM

ACKNOWLEDGMENTS

Janelle Millard, your research, organization, and ideas bring life to this book. Your commitment to this project and your attention to detail have been invaluable. Thank you!

Dr. Sharon Flinder, Dr. Garry Coleman, and Dr. Altyn Clark—your insights and anecdotes made this book more accessible, useful, and stimulating. You are cherished, my friends.

I appreciate TSI's talented employees, teaming partners, service providers, and clients. You inspire my work and motivate me to write books that help people unleash their potential.

The ForbesBooks team is truly stellar. You made this project a lot of fun, and your professionalism is second to none.

Many thanks to every individual who reads this

book. May you experience the joy of fully tapping into your many superpowers as you soar to new heights on your leadership journey.

ENDNOTES

Chapter 1

1 Judith M. Bardwick, *Danger in the Comfort Zone: From Boardroom to Mailroom—How to Break the Entitlement Habit That's Killing American Business*, (New York: American Management Association, 1991).

2 Ibid.

3 Ron Ashkenas, "To Increase Innovation: Help Your Team Take Smarter Risks," *Forbes*, March 2016, https://www.forbes.com/sites/ronashkenas/2016/03/21/to-increase-innovation-help-your-team-take-smarter-risks/#4c544611505d.

4 Lisa Feldman Barrett, "How to Become a Superager," *The New York Times*, December 2016, https://www.nytimes.com/2016/12/31/opinion/sunday/how-to-become-a-superager.html.

5 Ibid.

Chapter 2

1 Ed Catmull, "How Pixar Fosters Collective Creativity," *Harvard Business Review*, September 2008, https://hbr.org/2008/09/how-pixar-fosters-collective-creativity.

2 Kevin Daum, "18 Quotes on the Surprising Value of Losing," Inc., February 6, 2019, https://www.inc.com/kevin-daum/a-celebration-of-losing.html.

Chapter 3

1 "Employee engagement study shows enthusiasm has huge ROI," Dale Carnegie of Tennessee, December 3, 2012, www.dalecarnegietn.com/employee-engagement-study-shows-enthusiasm-has-huge-roi/.

2 Shawn Anchor, "The Happiness Dividend," *Harvard Business Review*, June 23, 2011, https://hbr.org/2011/06/the-happiness-dividend.

Chapter 4

1 Donald Sull, "Managing by Commitments," *Harvard Business Review*, June 2003, https://hbr.org/2003/06/managing-by-commitments.

2 "The Mayer-Salovey-Caruso Emotional Intelligence Test (MSCEIT)," Consortium for Research on Emotional Intelligence in Organizations, 2002, http://www.eiconsortium.org/measures/msceit.html.

3 Warren Berger, "Why Curious People Are Destined for the C-Suite," *Harvard Business Review*, September 11, 2015, https://hbr.org/2015/09/why-curious-people-are-destined-for-the-c-suite.

4 Tomas Chamorro-Premuzic, "Curiosity Is as Important as Intelligence," *Harvard Business Review*, August 27, 2014, https://hbr.org/2014/08/curiosity-is-as-important-as-intelligence.

5 Scott Barry Kaufman, "Schools Are Missing What Matters about Learning," *The Atlantic,* July 24, 2017, https://www.theatlantic.com/education/archive/2017/07/the-underrated-gift-of-curiosity/534573/.

6 Bill George, "Courage: The Defining Characteristic of Great Leaders," *Forbes*, April 24, 2017, https://www.forbes.com/sites/hbsworkingknowledge/2017/04/24/courage-the-defining-characteristic-of-great-leaders/#ad8591b11ca5.

7 Ben Dean, "Authentic Happiness," University of Pennsylvania, 2019, https://www.authentichappiness.sas.upenn.edu/newsletters/authentichappinesscoaching/courage.

8 Malala Yousafzai, *I Am Malala: The Girl Who Stood Up for Education and Was Shot by the Taliban* (London, Weidenfeld & Nicolson, 2013).

9 Melanie Greenberg, "The Six Attributes of Courage," *Psychology Today*, August 23, 2012, https://www.psychologytoday.com/us/blog/the-mindful-self-express/201208/the-six-attributes-courage.

Chapter 5

1 "Leader-Member Exchanges," Society for Industrial and Organizational Psychology, 1998, accessed March 20, 2019, http://www.siop.org/instruct/LMXTheory/sld003.aspx.

Chapter 6

1 "Conscious Capitalist Credo," Conscious Capitalism, accessed March 20, 2019, https://www.consciouscapitalism.org/about/credo.

2 Ibid.

Chapter 7

1 David G. Myers and C. Nathan DeWall, *Psychology,* 11th ed. (New York: Worth Publishers, 2015).

2 Mike Krzyzewski, "Coach K on How to Connect," *The Wall Street Journal*, July 16, 2011, https://www.wsj.com/articles/SB10001424052702303678704576441823130334218.

Chapter 8

1 Charles Duhigg, "What Google Learned from Its Quest to Build the Perfect Team," *The New York Times Magazine*, February, 25 2016, https://www.nytimes.com/2016/02/28/magazine/what-google-learned-from-its-quest-to-build-the-perfect-team.html.

Chapter 9

1 Gregory Korte, "Obama: Pat Summitt Was a Role Model for My Daughters," *USA Today*, (June 2016), https://www.usatoday.com/story/news/politics/theoval/2016/06/28/obama-pat-summitt-role-model-my-daughters/86466624/.

INDEX

ABOUT THE AUTHOR

Dr. Marta Wilson is an industrial-organizational psychologist and the CEO of Transformation Systems Inc. (TSI), an award-winning consulting firm that helps leaders be their best, do great things, and have meaningful success. Marta has dedicated her career to helping people and communities expand potential and boost effectiveness through her work as a leadership consultant, business author, keynote speaker, board member, and charity fundraiser.

Marta is the creator of LEAP, which stands for Leadership Effectiveness And Potential. LEAP is a framework and a program that includes assessments, keynotes, workshops, training, mentoring, learning reinforcers such as the LEAP app, and ongoing consulting and transformation support. This innovative program is implemented by organizations to lift entire workforces to new heights. With LEAP, thousands of people are discovering their unique superpowers and unleashing their inner superheroes.

As a speaker, Marta fuels change with her dynamic message and energizes her audiences to focus on achieving new peaks of performance. With a passion to share proven strategies that drive client results, Marta is the author of several books including *Energized Enterprise*, *Everybody's Business*, *Leaders in Motion*, and *The Transformation Desktop Guide*.

With Marta at the helm, TSI has received numerous accolades for helping set historic records in federal-acquisition processes and for facilitating large-scale technology transitions. In addition, TSI is recognized as one of the Washington Business Journal's Best Places to Work and has received the National Jefferson Award for Public Service, Society for Human Resource Management's Employer All-Star Award, and Virginia's Fantastic 50 Award. TSI also ranked on the Inc. 5000 list for five consecutive years as one of the fastest-growing private companies in America.

Recognized for leadership and service, Marta is named as one of the Washington Business Journal's Top 25 Women Business Leaders in DC and by the March of Dimes as a Heroine of Washington. She serves as the board secretary of the Northern Virginia Technology Council and as a board member of the Association for Corporate Growth National Capital Region. She is a board member and the former board chair of Easterseals DC MD VA and a member of the American Red Cross Tiffany Circle.

Marta holds PhD and MS degrees in industrial-organizational psychology from Virginia Tech and a BA in academic psychology from the University of Tennessee.